So Who's Stopping You

So Who's Stopping You

The Success Series

By Warren Greshes

Published 2018 by Gildan Media LLC
aka G&D Media
www.GandDmedia.com

FIRST EDITION 2018

Front Cover design by David Rheinhardt of Pyrographx

Interior design by Meghan Day Healey of Story Horse, LLC

Library of Congress Cataloging-in-Publication Data is available upon request

ISBN: 978-1-7225-0018-4

10   9   8   7   6   5   4   3   2   1

Contents

Introduction 1

Attitude and Commitment 3

The Secret to Keeping a Positive Attitude 15

The Three C's of Success 21

Fear of Failure 31

Someone Is Going to Say No 39

Setting Goals 55

Be Effective—Write It Down 67

Your Personal Action Plan 75

The Three Components of an Effective Plan.... 81

What the 21st Century Customer
Really Wants—Make My Life Easier 99

The Three S's of Success 127

About the Author 143

Introduction

Welcome to *So Who's Stopping You: The Success Series.* By choosing to read this, you've taken your first step to success. You'll find that the goal of this book is to help you create a focused direction and sense of purpose in your life, career, and business so that you can be as successful as you choose to be. This book contains no magic formulas, but I have tried my best to give you ideas, techniques, and solutions that are extremely easy to implement. In fact, they are so easy to implement that you will have no excuse not to do it.

In addition to being a pragmatic how-to look at personal and professional improvement, I think you'll enjoy the many stories and analogies that bring these points home. I have only given you ideas, solutions, and techniques that I know work, because I've tried each one of them.

You'll learn about such things as the importance of attitude and commitment; why you shouldn't let the fear of failure stop you; how to set goals and develop written action plans for your life, career, and business; how to differentiate yourself from the competition; the necessity of being able to act on your ideas; and why the quality of persistence is something you can't be without.

We start where everything starts, with your attitude and commitment, why it's important, and how we develop the kind of attitude and commitment that will enable us to be successful on into the future. So, get ready to learn something and have some fun at the same time, as you read *So Who's Stopping You: The Success Series.*

Attitude and Commitment

Did you ever walk down the street and see someone you know, who's a very depressing person? Now, you don't want to talk to that person. You see him or her coming towards you and every time you see them, all they have is a tale of woe. All they can talk about is how bad things are, how lousy they feel, or how awful everything is.

So you see this person coming towards you as you're walking down the street, and they don't see you, but you see them. What do you do? You probably duck into a store. You cover your face as you walk by, and make believe you're sneezing. I've seen a lot of women who carry those big bags, and they'll stick their head right in that bag, and make believe they're looking for something, just to avoid that person. Now, why do you do that? Because, you don't want to talk to that person, because, you don't want to talk to depressing people.

Now, on the other hand, did you ever walk down the street and see this person coming towards you, that always makes you feel good, a very up, very positive person? I'll bet you go out of your way to talk to him or her. (By the way, you know when you're in trouble? When you see that person cross to the other side of the street or hide his face. Then you know you've got big problems!) But, for our purposes here, you look to talk to that person. You want to meet that person. Why? Because, you want to talk to someone who feels good.

Let me tell you about attitude and commitment. People like to deal with people that make them feel good, and people run from people that make them feel bad, because no one wants to talk to depressing people. People don't like to talk to losers. Why do you think winning sports teams fill stadiums and losing sports teams can't give away tickets? It's because people don't want to associate with losers. People want to be part of a winning situation. And that's in life, that's in business, and that's going to be in your career.

The attitude and the commitment that you have will determine your success, and I'm talking about the way you feel about yourself, the way you feel about what you do for a living, the way you feel about who you are or what you do, the way you feel about your customers, the way you feel about the products and services you sell. Because if you don't believe in who you are and what you do, don't expect anyone else to believe it. And that's attitude. That's commitment.

That, by the way, is what our customers buy from us. They buy our attitude. They buy our commitment. And you know why? Because when you talk to them, that's what they see, that's what they hear, and that's what they feel. You know the interesting thing is, people don't hear words. We know that. We know that people don't listen. Anybody that has kids can tell you that. But you know what people hear? People hear your attitude. People hear your commitment. And that's the type of thing that they buy. They buy your attitude. They buy your commitment.

A friend of mine is also a professional speaker. His name is Wayne Pickering. He's an expert on health and wellness, and he always says, "Your attitude will determine your altitude."

I think one of the biggest questions I get from executives and from business owners is, "How do I find good people? When I'm looking to hire people, first and foremost, what do I look for?"

And I always tell them the same thing. "When you're looking to hire people the first thing you want to look for is attitude."

Because to be perfectly honest about it, you can teach people almost anything else that they need to know, but one of the toughest things to teach is attitude, because attitude and commitment have to come from within.

So, when you're looking to hire people, you've got to look for attitude. Let's face it, if you have a person with a lousy attitude and they have all the skills in the world, that's not going to help them. Somebody with great skills and no attitude doesn't use the skills. So, because they don't use them, they lose them.

Yet, if you have somebody with limited skills but a great attitude, you know as well as I do, that that is the kind of person who will run through brick walls to learn what they have to learn and the kind of person that will chase you to the ends of the earth in order to develop the skills that they need to be successful. And that's the kind of person you want working for you. So, hire attitude above everything else because attitude is where this all starts.

Where does this attitude and commitment come from, and what can we do to develop it in our lives, in our careers, and our businesses, and also in the people we lead, the people that work with us, the people that work for us, and maybe even in our kids?

I'll tell you, that's the tough part. I'm a motivational speaker, and I have inspired audiences all over the world. Somehow the toughest people I find to inspire are my own kids. My son thinks I'm boring, and he says, "Oh, Dad, I've heard all these stories before." I'm sure you hear the same thing from your kids.

Attitude and commitment have to be acquired. You're just not born with it. And one of the things I like to say is that we acquire our high level of attitude and commitment from the goals we establish in our lives. These two qualities are the basis for everything.

I used to work in the Garment Center in New York City. That's where I started as a salesperson, and became a sales manager. I started selling in the Garment Center in 1973, which is probably one of the worst periods of the last 40 or 50 years to start a sales career. 1973-74 in New York City was the height of the fiscal crisis and right smack in the middle of a pretty deep recession.

I was a sales manager and a salesman. And I'll never forget I had this salesperson working for me, who was one of the most depressing people I can ever remember. He didn't last very long, obviously, but he used to sit people down in our showroom, where we sold the dresses that we manufactured, and he would bring the line over. He'd say to a buyer, "Listen, I know business is bad, but I want to show you a few things anyhow."

Now, you talk about putting people in a bad frame of mind to do business; whereas, think about the salespeople with great attitudes, that they just put you in a perfect frame of mind to buy. This guy had such a hard time doing business because he was telling people right upfront there's no reason to buy, things are too bad. You keep telling people things are bad, they start believing it, whether it's true or not. On the other hand, when you're dealing with a salesperson who is positive, who's always upbeat, you like dealing with that person. You want to gravitate towards him.

I frequently travel in my business, and one of the things I often do, is rent cars. There are all sorts of car rental companies. There are cheap ones, and there are more expensive ones. Personally I use Avis, and one of the reasons I do is because I like the people that are on the phone. I like their attitude. It is outstanding. When I talk to them, they're always informative, they're always upbeat. I remember I started using Avis because they sent me a free membership in the mail to their Avis Wizards Club, which is an elite membership for frequent users. At the same time, Hertz sent me an elite membership too, so I had to choose between the two of them.

Now, I called Hertz to begin with, because obviously they're the more popular name, and I've got to tell you, their people on the phone, were just ordinary and I didn't enjoy talking to them very much. Their attitude was not great. They were a little curt on the phone; whereas, when I called Avis, they had a great attitude. So, I've been using Avis ever since, and that's been for many years, and it's all because of the way they dealt with me on the phone.

I live in Chapel Hill, North Carolina. We moved here from New York City a little over six years ago. One of the things I did when investigating the community that I wanted to live in was to look for a good local car service that could get me to and from the airport. My biggest concern when I go out to do a speech is actually getting there, not how good the speech is. I'm not worried about that. I'm more worried about getting there. If I don't get there, it doesn't matter how good the speech is.

Well, I got a Yellow Pages, and I started calling car services all around the Chapel Hill area, and most of them were just pretty ordinary, except for one, a company called Thorpe's. And the person I spoke to on the phone was just so nice, so helpful, and so informative that I couldn't help but do business with them.

And here it is six years later, and it's the only car service I've done business with since, strictly because of the way they handled themselves and the attitude that came through on the phone. They were positive. They were friendly. They were informative. They treated me as if I were important. They weren't looking to rush me off the phone, even though I wasn't calling to book any business with them.

The other car services I called made me feel like I was talking to someone who was walking backwards as they were speaking to me. So, here it is six years later, and I've been a longtime customer of Thorpe's, all because of their attitude.

So, when you're out there, I don't care who you're dealing with, your attitude will determine whether you will be successful or not.

My daughter is on a jump rope team, and her coach preaches attitude. I think it's one of the greatest lessons she's ever learned. I know jump roping is an unusual sport. I never heard of it until I moved down here to Chapel Hill, North Carolina. But I'll tell you something, she has really benefited from this coach, because he demands people have a good attitude. He demands people work hard. You are rewarded for having a good attitude. You are not rewarded for having a bad attitude and for not working hard.

By the way, speaking of attitude, I received an email from someone named, Max, saying "Mr. Greshes, my attitude can use altering, upgrading, and changing. I know it. But how? I don't seem to be able to get out of this funk I am in, and I feel like I am faking it if I pretend to be up and positive when I don't feel it in my bones. How can I change this?"

Well, that's a great question, and it's a problem that a lot of people have. One of the reasons that people have a bad attitude and why they don't seem to be able to get out of the funk that they're in, is because they really have no sense of purpose. They have no particular direction in their life or their career. So, what I would suggest to people like Max, is to start to put together some goals. Sit down and figure out if you are where you want to be? Are you doing what you want to do? Where do you want to be? What do you want to do? What do you want to do with your life and your career? Start writing some things down. Start to figure out a new sense of purpose for yourself and figure out what it is you want to do with your life, what it is you want to do with your career.

Commitment only comes from being committed to something. You have to be committed to something to have a good attitude. When you wake up in the morning and you don't like your job, we've all been there. I've worked jobs I hated. There is no worse prison than working in a job that you hate, because you just feel aimless. And so my suggestion to you is to really figure out what you want to do with your life, what you want to do with your career, and really try to focus. In other words, where do I want to be? What do I want to do? Am I doing what I want to do? And how can I do it?

Start writing things down. If you're not going to be committed enough to write something down, then you're certainly not going to be committed enough to doing it.

I really think that attitude is everything. I think you've got to get up in the morning and decide what your attitude is for the day. There are people who actually count their blessings every morning, and then ask themselves what they want to make things better. It's like a mantra every morning. These meditations are called affirmations.

Most people are not successful. That's why success is so easy. You know why—because there's so little competition. But if you visualize something that you really want and then go after it, they say that you're more likely to get it. Visualizing your life being what it is you want it to be.

I always say if you can see yourself successful, you can be successful. In other words, if you can see yourself doing something in your mind, then you can do it. But if you can't even see yourself doing something in your mind, how can you be able to do it in real life?

Of course, there are points along the way when each of us gets a little tired. You know, we've been pushing. We've been thinking positive thoughts. We've been doing our affirmations, and then you get up one morning and you go, "The heck with this. I'm tired." How do you get through that part?

Well, you know what, taking a rest for a day or so is not going to kill you. But with your goals and your dreams, you constantly have to be reevaluating because sometimes what you think you wanted three months ago, three months later is not that important to you.

How do you trust your next instinct? You know what, you've just got to. I've got a friend, and he's a very bright businessman. People always say well, he's so lucky, his ideas all turn to gold. And you know what he says to me?

He says, "You know why I'm so lucky? Because I try so many ideas. They don't see the ones that don't work."

It's like in selling, the first lesson I ever learned is if you chop enough wood, the chips have got to fall somewhere. I was watching an interview with Larry King, and we all look at him as being the epitome of success. But he's had a lot of failures along the way. He's filed bankruptcy twice.

Well, you know what; one of the keys to success is to fail a lot. It's not how often you fall down, it's how often you get up.

I'm sure you want your children to have commitment and the right attitude, but like I said, it's hard to get them to listen to you.

We know we should work because of the example passed down by our parents. In other words, I know I've got to go to work every day, and I've got to make a living, and I've got to support my family, because I watched my father do that. I watched my father get up every morning, go to work. It didn't matter if he was sick. It didn't matter if he didn't feel like going that day. My father got up every day, he went to work, he never took a day off, and he supported his family. So, right away, that's a lesson that kids learn. They learn from watching you.

If you have a great work ethic, your kids will get that from you. But now the next thing we need to do to instill that work ethic in our kids is we've got to make them work, starting with chores around the house. My son is now 16. Last summer he was still 15, and before the summer, I said to him, "Michael, guess what, you're getting a job this summer. Whether you want to or not, you're getting a job. It's time."

I gave him a choice. I said, "Now, you can either work a job for somebody else every single day or you can come up with an idea for your own business."

And you know what, since he didn't feel like working every day, he said, "You know, I can make money, work less, and have my own business." So, he started a business. My son's a baseball player. He plays high school baseball. He made up fliers, and he started a business giving lessons to kids.

He gave lessons to kids anywhere from the age of 7 to 12 years old. He got himself a bunch of clients, making about ten bucks an hour. He worked all summer doing that. Then he socked away all of his money, and he invested it too. I taught him how to invest in the stock market, so he's been investing his money. When he does something, he likes being able to get paid for it. He wants to do more of that.

He's been taking many business courses in high school. My daughter, luckily, is on the jump rope team where work ethic is everything. And if you're not willing to work you're not going to reap the benefits of being on this team, which is all about the travel and the competitions and the championships. So, she's learning work ethic through her coach. The problem is there are a lot of bad coaches out there. But there are some good ones too, and you've got to find them.

I think both the example you set and sometimes holding their feet to the fire, are great at making children want to work hard. I remember when I used to say to my father, "Dad, can I get a new baseball glove?" He'd say, "Sure." He'd pause for about five seconds, and then he'd say, "As soon as you save up for it."

It's amazing, but work ethic is something that you don't see a lot of out there. In fact, we're amazed that the work ethic doesn't prevail in today's marketplace. A friend was having her house painted and was very surprised at how the painters just didn't seem to care about the job they were doing. We find that so often. It's so hard to find people who want to do a good job, and when you find one, it's even harder because they're in such demand.

The Secret to Keeping a Positive Attitude

I am often asked "How do you bring your attitude up when you are feeling down?" For the most part, I'm a very positive person with a winning attitude, but once in a while it does get down, and it is hard to bring it back up. I try to bring myself up by looking at the positive of everything.

I'll tell you what my secret is. I like doing this. This is fun. I love doing radio shows. This happens to be a great day for me, simply because this has been a goal of mine for many years, to get my own radio show, and now I have it. When we work towards things we really want, that enables us to keep our attitude up.

We have to constantly be setting new challenges for ourselves. Whenever we feel that we're getting into a rut, whenever we feel that we're in a lull, and even if you're a positive person, you can get down. I've been there. I've been down too. I think you have to start setting new challenges for yourself.

When I worked in the Garment Center, I had gotten to the point after about seven, eight years of doing it that I just didn't want to do it anymore. I could see that I didn't want to do this for the rest of my life. I was one of those people that would walk around all day and say, "God, I hate doing this. Oh, I don't want to do this anymore, but there's nothing else I can do, so I might as well stay because they pay me well." I was making a lot of money, and I'm a good salesman. But I got to the point where I was working one day a week, and the rest of the time I was reading a newspaper or spacing out. I just couldn't see myself living that kind of existence for the next 30 years.

And so instead of saying constantly to myself, "There's nothing else I can do," finally one day I woke up and said, "You know, there is something else I can do. My problem is I haven't bothered to get off my rear end and figure out what it is. When I do get off of my rear end and figure out what it is, then I'm going to energize myself." And that is what happened. I got up off my butt, figured out what it was I wanted to do with my life, and even though I hadn't gotten there yet, just the action of figuring out what I wanted to do with my life, setting that new challenge in front of me, energized me so much. I had never been so energized in my life.

Then I learned how to set goals, which energized me even more. And I think that's the secret. You've got to be putting new challenges in front of yourself every single day.

I received an email from Bob from Minnesota a couple of weeks ago who said, "I firmly believe that attitude can be a choice that we make every day. I've heard others talk about attitude, but I would really like to hear your take on it."

Like I said, when I worked the job I hated I didn't feel like getting up in the morning, but when I finally sat down and figured out what I wanted to do with my life and put some new challenges in front of me, it was amazing. I had never felt so energized before in my life.

I went and sought help, not psychological help. The first thing I did was to go to a career counseling company, not even with the thought of them doing any counseling on me. I went because I needed a resume written. Can you believe that? Here I was, I had four years of college. I had worked in the business world for ten years. I didn't even know how to write a resume. In the Garment Center, you don't write resumes. Basically you write down what you did on a cocktail napkin, tie it to a rock, and throw it through someone's window.

So, here I am, looking for a resume. I go to this place figuring I'm just going to pay them to write a resume for me, and I'm out of here. Well, they sold me the whole line of career counseling services. I think at the time, back in 1982-83, it cost me about $1,000, which seemed like a lot of money.

Folks, one of the biggest obstacles you're ever going to find to success is other people, because other people are always going to tell you that all your ideas are crazy. Of course, people told me, "$1,000 on that, you must be nuts." I thought about it, and I said, "First of all, it's tax deductible. Second of all, I could go on vacation and blow $2,000, $3,000, and what have I got for it? Some photos, and that's about it," although not even that, because I don't usually take pictures when I go on vacation.

So, I paid the $1,000, and I have to tell you, it was the best $1,000 I ever spent in my life. These people put me through a process that really made me focus. They asked me all sorts of questions, and it really made me focus on what I wanted to do with my life. They said, "Do you want to stay in sales?" And I said, "Yes, I like selling. I'm good at selling. I want to do something I'm good at, and I like it, and that's what I want to do."

They said, "Do you want to sell a product or a service?" I said, "Well, I want to sell a service. Because I've sold a product for so many years, I want to sell a service." "What kind of a service?" I said, "I want to sell a service that almost any kind of company can use." Because I had been in such a narrow industry, this was an exciting new direction.

By asking me all these questions, they boiled it down for me. With all the answers, we focused on four different industries, one of them being the sales training industry. I got a job selling sales training services, worked for a sales training company, and did a lot of business for them. I've got to tell you, the first day I was on that job, it felt like I had been there my whole life. Why? Because I created that job. I wrote down what I wanted. I created it. I researched it. I created it, and so it was fantastic from the first day I was there. I spent a couple years there and went to every sales training session I could. I watched. I learned, and eventually I decided I was going to start my own business, and that's what I did and how I did it.

So, the challenges you put in front of yourself are really what gets you going every day, creating that focus, creating that direction, creating that sense of purpose in both your life and your career, and a lot of it comes from the commitments we make.

The Three C's of Success

I like to talk about what I call the three C's of success. They are commitment, courage, and confidence. Basically that's the progression. Commitment is the first thing you need. People are always worried about doing something new, doing something different because they're not confident. You can't be confident in something if you've never done it before. In other words, the commitment to "This is what I want to do, and this is what I need to do, and this is what I'd love to do" will give me the courage to act. And once I've acted; well, now I'm committed. Now I feel good. Now I feel like I can conquer the world.

Let me give you an example. For those of you who are in sales, do you remember making that first sales call? Remember that first cold call? Now, I'll bet you were nervous before you did it. I bet you weren't real confident that you could do it. I mean, let's face it, cold calls are not easy. They're not fun. But the commitment to the fact that this is what you wanted to do, the commitment to the fact that this is what you had to do gave you the courage to make that call. And after it was over, what did you say to yourself? You said, "Hey, that wasn't so bad. I can do that. I'll do it again."

So, now you have the confidence. See, confidence only comes from doing. How can you be confident in your ability to do something if you've never done it before? The commitment's the first thing. Unless you have the commitment, you're not going to be confident in your ability to do things. So, the commitment gives us the confidence to act, and once we act, the commitment gives us the courage to act. Then we do it, and now we're confident.

Do any of you ski? I'm not a skier. I'm not a big snow sports type of guy. I don't like the cold weather. But did you ever ski? You're standing at the top of the hill, you're looking down, you're thinking, "Oh man, I don't want to do this." But the commitment to the fact that you have to do it, and the biggest reason you have to do it is because the chair lift only goes up, it doesn't go down. So, you go down the mountain. Everybody's calling you chicken. You go down the mountain, you get to the bottom of the hill, and you say, "Hey, that wasn't so bad. Now I feel confident I can do it."

Like I said, I spent the first part of my business career in the Garment Center, and one of the single biggest reasons I got out of there was it was one of the most negative industries I had ever been involved in. To this day, it still is.

I've been out of the garment center since 1983, and sometime around 1993, I got a call from one of my booking agents, who said we have someone who's interested in you speaking to them. I said, "Well, who is it?" They said it was Sears. I said, "Oh, Sears, that's interesting. I used to sell dresses to them." They said, "Well, that's exactly why they want you. The audience is going to be all dress manufacturers."

I said, "Well, you've got to hire me." I said, "I'm probably the only motivational speaker in America who's ever been in the dress business." They said, "That's exactly why they want to hire you. They decided you're the only speaker that this audience won't walk out on." The people in the Garment Center are convinced that nobody knows anything except them. I can't understand why they think that since their business has been so bad for the last 30 years.

So I went. It was just incredible. There were people in the audience I hadn't seen in ten years, my old boss who broke me into the business, which was great because I made fun of him during my speech, and they all laughed, which was fantastic. Afterwards, everybody was coming up to me saying, "Oh, you're so lucky you got out of the business. This business stinks. You're so lucky you got out." And I'm saying to myself, "My God, this tone hasn't changed in over ten years," and it hasn't changed to this date, people saying you're so lucky. There's no luck involved. Luck has nothing to do with it. Anybody can do it.

If I did it, anybody can do it. That's what I'll tell anybody who calls in and anybody who's listening to this show is that no matter what it is in your life, you can do it; you've just got to figure out what it is. The single biggest reason people are not successful in their lives is because they never bother to figure out what it is that they want, and that's one of the reasons their attitude is so bad.

I get managers and business owners often saying to me, "If I could only find the right button to push on this guy, then I could motivate him." But the real problem is this, it's not finding the right button to push, it's the fact that the guy has no buttons. How do you push the right button on someone who doesn't have a button? The single biggest reason that people are not self-motivated is because they themselves don't know what motivates them.

So, if any of you are managers or business owners, who have people reporting to you, the first thing you need to do, your first job with any of your people is to help them find their buttons. If they can't find their buttons, since they don't know what motivates them, then they're not going to come to work with a great attitude every day.

In the business world, the attitude of the people that deal with the customers is the most important thing. Your people in your front line are dealing with customers every day. If they don't have a good attitude, then the chain is broken, and so the key is to help these people find their buttons, help them figure out what motivates them.

If you can help a person figure out what it is that motivates them, why they're coming to work every day, what they are working for, then even if they hate the job, they still come to work with a better attitude because now they're working for themselves. They have now learned how they can use the job as a vehicle towards getting themselves what they want.

I've been a professional speaker now for over 18 years and I'm amazed at how many corporate meetings I've keynoted where I've sat in the audience and watched the CEO or some big executive get up there and say, "If we work really hard this year, we put our noses to the grindstone and we really do our best, this company will do great." I look at hundreds if not thousands of people sitting there in the audience with that expression on their face that says, "Who cares?" Because what do they want to know? They want to know what's in it for me.

The biggest problem is not that they want to know what's in it for me; the biggest problem is this, is that if I ask those people, "What would you like to be in it for you?" they really couldn't answer me because they don't know what it is that they want. Everything stems from this. See, the attitude, the commitment, it all starts here, and if we don't have that great attitude, if we don't have that sense of purpose, if we don't know what it is that we want to be in it for us, how can we get excited about it? If we're working just for somebody else, how can we get excited about it? But if we're working for us, then we get excited, then we want to get out there, then we want to do stuff.

So, that's the key. The key is to figure out what it is you want for you, to figure out what your buttons are. And for you managers and business owners out there, that's your job, to help your people find their buttons.

I'm a big sports fan. If you are interested at all in sports and are any kind of a fan, have you ever noticed how many athletes with talent never make it and how many with limited talent make it big and the biggest difference is their attitude? We see that all the time.

There's a player for the California Angels, for the Anaheim Angels, David Eckstein. David Eckstein is a shortstop for the California Angels, and he's about five foot nothing, weighs about a hundred and nothing. He wasn't even given a scholarship in college to play baseball. I think he went to Florida State or University of Florida, one of those schools, and he wasn't even asked to play on the team, but he would be in the batting cage every day practicing and practicing and practicing. The coach finally saw him and saw this kid that was working so hard. He asked if he wanted to practice with the team, and this kid worked so hard and practiced so hard, he was practicing and working harder than anybody else, they put him on the team.

Here's a guy that wasn't even good enough to make a college team, and now he's playing in the Major Leagues strictly on his work ethic, his attitude, his commitment. So, this is what he wanted to do. I hate David Eckstein because his Angels beat my Giants in the 2002 World Series, game six, one of the worst days of my life, but here's a guy with limited talent, and he's a Major League Baseball player.

If you know anything about baseball, you know that his talent is next to nothing, and his attitude is everything. You get players in their careers like a Darryl Strawberry who had as much talent as anybody I'd ever seen and basically threw it away and did not have the work ethic of a David Eckstein or many other players that you see today with limited talent. So, the attitude is everything, and it's critical.

Customer Service Diary

This story is from one of my favorite segments on the radio show, what I called the *customer service diary*. I asked my listeners for their best and worst customer service stories so we could share and discuss them.

This great story came from Paul in Connecticut. "Here's a classic story and true. If you rent a car from National, they put both keys on a key ring that is wired shut so that you cannot remove either key. You only need one key to operate the vehicle. The keychain says it is a white vehicle, license plate so-and-so. There is no reference to National on the keychain. So, if a person lost a set of keys and someone else found them, they would not have a clue as to how to tie these back to the owner of the vehicle.

With today's cars, if you lose a set of keys, it will cost you between $200 and $300 to replace them. The car may have to be towed to the dealer, and that's another $80. That's because there are only two keys to the car, and both of them are on the same key ring."

He said, "But this happened to a college friend of mine last week. Fortunately, she was telling us the story as well as others when someone mentioned that they saw a set of keys lying behind the front desk at the hotel. Sure enough, it was the keys to the car, and the $400 expense was avoided."

"Now," Paul goes onto say, "when I turned in my rental car, I asked why the two keys are on the same ring when in fact you only need one to operate the car. I also asked why there is no notice on the key tag that says 'If found, call National at toll-free number so-and-so.'"

"The gal replied, 'Gee, you're about the 100th person to ask me that. I don't know why we do that. It's just the way it is.'"

Paul wrote, "Now, I am not a smart man, but after the sixth person asking me this question, I think I would have referred it onto management as a suggestion as how to better service the customer and become more user friendly. I wonder how many keys are sitting in a lost and found with no way of getting them back to the rightful owner at the tune of $300 each. Regards, Paul."

Isn't that great? That *is* a classic, and Paul is right, but you have to wonder where the real problem lies, since changing this policy makes so much sense. There has to be numerous reasons for this absurdity. Changing the system with the keys is a great idea, and it's amazing to me how many companies do things like this.

Changing the system with the keys is a great idea, but people are probably thinking it's too hard to implement, and when it comes to making a choice between doing the hard or doing the easy, most people and most companies will always do the easy. Management doesn't care enough, or maybe the people on the front line don't care enough and don't think this is a big enough problem to tell it to management. Or maybe, I'll give you a better one, and this happens too often in too many companies, the people on the front line are tired of going to management with good ideas or suggestions only to see nothing done about it. Nothing demoralizes a worker and their attitude more than constantly seeing their good ideas shot down.

Fear of Failure

I'll be talking about the single biggest reason people do not succeed, and it's because they are afraid to fail. You will learn why falling down is not the same as failing, why you should stop doing what everyone else does, and how to turn negatives into positives. Read on and learn, and most of all, do something about it.

Unfortunately, fear of failure is without a doubt the single biggest obstacle to success in the world, and the single biggest reason people don't succeed is because they are afraid to fail.

About ten years ago I read an article in the *Wall Street Journal*, about an area in Chicago. Teachers there were asked what to do with children who failed third grade, and the prevailing attitude among these teachers was that they should be passed on to fourth grade rather than be held back for fear of stigmatizing these kids.

This is incredible to me, something I don't understand at all. First of all, let's talk about the difference between failing and not passing. If a child fails third grade but repeats it and then passes third grade, did they really fail or did they just not pass the first time around?

It's not unlike the driver's license. I'm sure most of you have driver's licenses, and I'm sure not every single one of you passed your driving test the first time around. It is always interesting to me when people say I failed the driving test the first time I took it. And I say, "Well, did you really fail it?" You have a license. You didn't really fail. You just didn't pass.

I believe you fail the test when you fail it and don't take it again. In other words, the only time we ever really fail is when we stop trying. So, does a kid who fails the third grade really fail if they come back again, pass it, and move on?

The next question is about the logic of putting children in the fourth grade if they can't do third grade work? Teachers say it stigmatizes them to leave them back, but in the long run is it really helping them to pass them on if they can't do the work? How stigmatized will they be when they get out into the real world and can't compete at all?

Instead, why not encourage these kids to repeat the third grade, and when they pass, applaud the achievement, make it a positive instead of being a negative? Instead of being stigmatized, wouldn't that energize them to attack the next obstacle that comes their way? If you just pass them on after they've so-called failed, just like with people, aren't you really teaching them that every time they reach an obstacle, don't worry, somebody else is going to take care of it for you? Because that's not how it works in real life.

So, instead of stigmatizing them, energize them to attack the next obstacle that comes their way. How is failure handled where you work? When someone "fails" at a task, and I'm putting quotes around that word fail, how do you handle it? Do you treat it as a failure or do you treat it as a falling down?

Go ice skating, people are always interesting when they go ice skating. You come back, you ask, "How did you do?" "Oh, I did great. I didn't fall." Well, does not falling mean that you're a good ice skater, or does not falling mean that you never let go of the rail?

We're going to fall down when we try to go beyond, when we try to break through our barriers. We're always going to fall down. The key to life is not trying not to fall down. The key to life is always getting up, because as long as you keep getting up, you always have a shot. The difference between success and failure is: how are you at dealing with obstacles?

Instead of getting annoyed at people, do we show them the correct situation? And when they do it over successfully, do we applaud them? This encourages people to try new things. If you encourage people to get up and keep going, it's going to encourage people to always try different things, to not be afraid.

At the end of this *Wall Street Journal* article about kids so-called failing the third grade, a teacher asked, very defiantly, "How many adults will get up and keep going after they have failed?" And my response to that is "only the successful ones."

What kind of lesson are we teaching our kids if every time they fall down, we tell them it is okay, they don't have to bother getting up? What kind of lesson are we teaching ourselves every time we do that?

The interesting thing about most people that are afraid to fail is they're more afraid about what other people will think. I've got to tell you, other people are probably the single biggest obstacle to your success. People are always worried if I fail, what are other people going to think? Other people, I wouldn't worry about them. You can't live your life worrying about what other people think.

When I graduated from college, the first thing I did that summer was to work in a car wash. After having a four-year degree from college, I was well-qualified to work at a car wash. It was a very educated car wash too. We had people with college degrees. We had people with master's degrees.

It wasn't the greatest time for employment in America, but it was a fun job for the summer. I saved up all the money I could, and in September of 1972, I put a pack on my back and I split. I went to Europe, and I spent about four or five months in Europe. And before I left, I was telling people all about my trip and how long I was going to go. I'll never forget how many people said to me, "It's great that you're doing this now because once you get older you're never going to have this chance again." And that scared the living heck out of me.

All I could think of was, "My God, here I am, I'm 21 years old. Is my life over?" I never believed that. To this day, I never believed that. I never believed it back then. I don't believe it now. I said I'm going to prove all these people wrong, and I have.

In my life, I have chosen to pack up and go when I felt like it. I've had the opportunity to travel all over the world through my business and for pleasure too. When you don't think this way, it's almost like putting yourself in a mental prison that you're going to conform to what everybody else wants of you because you're afraid to break out of the box. Never be afraid to break out of the box.

A long time ago I heard that the quickest way to succeed is to look at what everybody else is doing and do something totally different. I'll never forget that trip and the reaction of people that to this day still say that, you're lucky you did it then because when you get older, you're never going to be able to do that again. Well, I have done that again, and I know lots of people who have done that again.

If you're afraid to fail, you're never going to succeed. Take that first step. Create your goals, folks. That's probably one of the biggest things that you can do—create your goals. When you have a really focused sense of purpose, it's going to be a lot easier to go ahead. It's going to be a lot harder for other people to stop you.

Customer Service Diary

Here is a great question from Jim from Summerfield, North Carolina who asked "How do you make the first step in making the change from secure full-time employment to starting your own business, concerns of family, well-being, mortgages, payments, etc.?"

That's a great question, and something I'm familiar with because I went through the process myself when I started my own business. That's a big problem for a lot of people. It's not an easy thing to do, for any of you contemplating the same thing.

You have a job. You're secure in your job, and you're getting that weekly paycheck. You have real strong urges to start your own business, and starting your own business, to me, is always one of the greatest things you can possibly do. It was one of the greatest things I've ever done in my life and one of the most rewarding things I've ever done. Starting your own business is really something that's great, but the problem is that there are concerns.

You have a family, you have that secure income, and you're saying to yourself, "What am I going to do if something goes wrong?" See, this is where the fear of failure comes in. The first thing people think of is, "What happens if something goes wrong?" rather than, "What happens if something goes right?" Why don't we ever think of that first? Why don't we ever think I can, rather than I can't?

Jim, let me tell you a couple things you can do to get the ball rolling. First of all, pick a time when you want to start your business. Shoot for a specific time. Set a goal that I'm 21 going to start my business in a year, two years, three years, whatever it may be. Know very positively what that business is going to be. Be real clear and specific on what that business is going to be, and set a timeframe.

From now until that timeframe is up, you want to get your financial affairs in order. Start first with getting your overhead in order. You want your overhead to be as low as it can possibly be. You want your expenses to be as low as they can possibly be. No unnecessary spending of any kind. I want you to save as much money as you can possibly save. If your spouse is working, I want her to save as much money as she can possibly save, and really sock it away and invest it wisely, because you're going to need that money.

The problem with starting your own business is that when you start a business, the last thing that ever comes is the money. You can't go into business worrying about making money because making money is the last thing that's going to happen. You go into business worrying about doing something that you want to do, that you love to do, and doing it the best way you can possibly do it.

So, my advice to you is to get your finances in order, to really cut down on the expenses. Eating out, cut it down to the bone. Vacations, cut them down to the bone. I know these are things you like to do, but my theory is always think long term—short-term pain for long-term gain.

Always think long-term. I learned that a long time ago. So, get those financial ducks in a row, get your overhead down to the bare minimum, and then plan out when you want to start that business and get as much money behind you as you can because you're going to need it.

Financing is tough for a brand new business. I don't think banks are going to talk to you. I know if it's a service business, then you're pretty much looking at borrowing from your credit card somewhere down the road as I did. But you never want to be using your credit cards for unnecessary things. Get yourself as debt free as you possibly can. I don't mean your mortgage, but other debts debt free as you possibly can, and I think you'll be successful. I don't see any problem in that.

Someone Is Going to Say No

Most people, and especially salespeople, don't like to make the calls. Salespeople don't like to make calls because they are afraid someone is going to say no. And they are right. Someone *is* going to say no. I say, who cares? Someone has to say no. If you've never heard no in your life, then you've probably never heard the word yes either. Let me remind you that the most successful salespeople in America are the ones that fail more often than anybody else. Why? It's because they speak to more people than anybody else, and that's why they fail the most.

So, we are talking about fear of failure. We're talking about falling down versus failing. We're talking about not being afraid to fail. We're talking about covering your behind rather than being willing to succeed. Are you just looking to do okay, or are you looking to succeed? Are you looking to not fail, or are you looking to succeed? That's what I find with a lot of people. A lot of salespeople are afraid to make the calls.

Here is a great example of what I'm talking about. This is the story about a man who made it into the *Guinness Book of World Records* for selling. He sold the single largest life insurance policy on record, a policy with a death benefit of $100 million on the life of entertainment entrepreneur, David Geffen.

Peter Rosengard was his name. He worked for a company in England called Abbey Life. Amazingly, he sold this policy off of a cold call. Why? It's because Peter was not afraid to fail. He knew what he wanted, and he just went out there and he did it.

He saw an article in the paper years ago about the MCA Corporation, a big entertainment company. He saw that MCA had just bought Geffen Records for something like $600 million. That's right, $600 million. He says to himself, "This is a fantastic deal." He knew something about the entertainment industry. And he also said to himself, "And I know that David Geffen is the single-most indispensable and driving force behind Geffen Records."

He knew that if something ever happened to David Geffen, the $600 million deal goes right down the drain. Therefore, "They need protection. They need life insurance."

Think about this. The average person is going to say to himself, "Why bother? After all, that's a big company; they're not going to talk to me. They probably have dozens of people on the payroll that take care of these things."

I asked Peter that question. "Did you even think of that?" And, "What were you thinking?" He said, "All

I can think of is these people have exposure. They have a problem. They need protection. They need life insurance. Heck, I sell life insurance. They might as well buy it from me. They're going to buy it from someone. They might as well buy it from me."

So, he decides to cold call the MCA Corporation. Even if the average salesperson gets this far, who do you think the average person is going to call at MCA? The average person is going to call personnel or perhaps the benefits department, the insurance department. You know as well as I do, if you've ever called personnel at any large company, they all have the same phone number: 1-800-BRICKWALL.

But not Peter, who decides he's going to call Sidney Sheinberg, the president of all of MCA. He gets on the phone, and he calls America. He calls information. He gets the main switchboard number of MCA. He calls the switchboard at MCA and says "Sid Sheinberg's office, please." Phone rings. Guess what happens. No, Sid Sheinberg doesn't answer. He gets the secretary. So, he leaves a message with the secretary because he finds out Sid Sheinberg's not in, leaves a message with the secretary, and he hangs up.

Now, think about this. At this point, even if the average person gets anywhere near this far, what do you think the average person does? That's right, he probably gives up. He probably doesn't even try to call again. Why? The average person is not really that concerned with succeeding. The average person is a lot more concerned with *not failing*. As long as he made the call, he's covered. That is the attitude of most people. As long as I've made that call, I'm covered, because if my boss asks me what's going on, I can always say I tried, I made that call. He's not in. That guy is never in. People like him don't speak to people like me.

But not Peter—Peter kept calling and calling and calling, because leaving a message and not getting through is not failing. Leaving a message and not getting through is falling down. Remember, you only fail by falling down if you don't get up. Peter got up, kept calling, calling, calling, never gets through. Eventually he did something really smart. Smart and cost effective—he got friendly with the secretary.

He got friendly with that secretary at MCA, and because he got friendly with that secretary, one day he finds out from the secretary that Sid Sheinberg is not in. But this time he finds out that Sid Sheinberg is in Italy on business. He finds out what town he's in. Now, he doesn't get the hotel out of her, but he finds out the town, and he knows the country. And now, the search was on. Because you know what Peter had? Peter had a window of opportunity.

Let me tell you something about windows of opportunity. Windows of opportunity are all around you, and the great thing is that windows of opportunity open up for you every single day. But the bigger problem is that windows of opportunity open up very quickly. They open up just a crack, and then *wham!* They close just as fast. Peter had this window and he just jumped right in. But let me back up and tell you a little more about Peter.

I told you that Peter sells life insurance, and now I'll tell you how he does it, which is through breakfast appointments. In fact, Peter would have a breakfast appointment every single day. Some days he would have two, three, four breakfast appointments. This guy ate more breakfast than anybody I know, and he'd always have that breakfast appointment at the Carlisle Hotel in London, a major five-star European hotel. I don't know if you know anything about major five-start European hotels, but at major five-star European hotels the concierges all retire as millionaires. Why? Because they don't get $2 tips. They get $2,000 tips.

So Peter is eating breakfast at this hotel every day, and because of that, he gets friendly with the concierge at the Carlisle Hotel. One day he finds out from him that all the concierges of all the five-star hotels in Europe all belong to the same club. So, he asks the concierge at the Carlisle, "If I was one of the single biggest executives at one of the single biggest entertainment companies in the world and I was staying at this particular town in Italy, what hotel would I stay at?" And the concierge said, "Well, there could be only one." He told him the hotel, and he said, "Do you happen to know the concierge at that hotel?" He said, "Of course. We belong to the same club." Talk about a window of opportunity. So now, Peter's got to make a call.

So no, you know you just don't make a call, cold. You've got to really think about it and know what you're going to say ahead of time, because you know as well as I do that you only get one shot at a first impression.

Peter thought about it and also thought about when the best time was to call, because he really needed to catch him. So he said to himself, "I know when these executives come to Europe that they all dress for dinner." Dinner is about 7:30-8:00. Cocktails are at 6:30. He thought if I call his room at about 5:30 in the afternoon, not only do I catch him in, but I just might catch him standing there in his underwear."

Now Peter decides he's going to make that call. He calls that hotel in Italy. Switchboard answers, "Sid Sheinberg's room, please." Phone rings, and now guess what happens. Sid picks up, "Sid Sheinberg, here." I want you to think about this now, folks, because here you are. You've got this shot. Remember, the average person is afraid to fail, afraid someone's going to say no. If the average person actually gets this far what do you think he says at this point?

Probably something like humina, humina, humina, humina, humina, you know the old Ralph Kramden routine. And you know why? Because the average person never believes that this kind of stuff is going to happen to them. They don't see themselves successful. They only see themselves failing. They're more afraid to fail than they're afraid to do something right. They're always worried about what could go wrong rather than what could go right.

But not Peter—calmly and quickly, Peter said, "Mr. Sheinberg, Peter Rosengard here from Abbey Life in London. Mr. Sheinberg, congratulations on that shrewd deal of buying Geffen Records for $600 million." I thought that was a pretty smart thing to say. Don't you think that Sid Sheinberg wants to be told he did something smart? Doesn't everybody?

Besides, what do you think the media was probably saying about the deal when it was first done? What do the media say about every deal when it's first done? They always say the same thing. They always say "paid too much," which I guess is the media's job because to me the media's job is to be negative at all times.

The media always says that, and then you know what's interesting? Five years later, they always say the same thing, "Boy, was that guy lucky to get that so cheap," which if we think about it, is why the people that write the articles never seem to be quite as successful as the ones who make the deals.

Everybody wants to be told they did something good. So Peter said, "Congratulations on that shrewd deal of buying Geffen Records for $600 million," and Sid Sheinberg thanked him. Then he said, "Thank you. What do you want?" And Peter said, "Well, Mr. Sheinberg, while buying Geffen Records for $600 million was a very shrewd deal, you know as well as I do that David Geffen is the single, driving, indispensable force behind Geffen Records. Did you ever think of what might happen to your $600 million investment should something happen to David Geffen?"

What do you think one of the single biggest executives at one of the single biggest entertainment companies in the world said? He said, "Gee, we never thought of that. What did you have in mind?" Whoa! Talk about a window of opportunity.

Even if the average person gets anywhere near this far—and like I said, most people are totally average. They'll do the same thing every single day, whether it works or not. Even if the average person gets anywhere near this far, what kind of a number you think the average person comes up with? They're probably going to come up with something like $2 or $5 million, because that sounds like big number to the average person.

But I want you to think about this. You are speaking to a man who has just written a check for $600 million. To this guy, a million dollars is a tip. Yet the average person has a huge fear of large numbers, because he never believes those kinds of numbers could ever be a part of his life, because he's more afraid to fail than looking forward to succeeding.

But not Peter—very calmly and very quickly, he said, well, I thought $100 million would be a great place to start. And the man that had just written a check for $600 million said, "Well, that sounds reasonable to me. Let's get it done." You know, folks, sometimes it is that easy, but you've got to give it a shot. You've got to try. He said to Peter, he said, "I want you to call this number tomorrow. You tell my assistant what you told me, and let's get this deal done."

And folks, months later, after all the underwriting, after all the papers were filled out, after all the medical exams, after they ran it past what I call the "sales prevention department," Peter Rosengard signed that deal for the $100 million life insurance policy and got himself into the *Guinness Book of World Records*. Why? It's because he never assumed. He never prejudged. He was not afraid to fail. He saw a prospect with a need. That's all he saw. He saw someone who needed what he had, and the only thing he could think of was they need what I have. They will get it from someone. They might as well buy it from me. He tried. Even when he fell down, he kept getting up.

Customer Service Diary

Paul from the UK: "I find that in the UK, much of the problem is caused by the preoccupation of the press on negative news; they seem to love the sniff of bad news." Paul, I've got to tell you something, it's not much different over here in the US either. In fact, it's the same thing.

He said, "This focuses many people on the negative instead of the good things in life." Let's face it, there are not too many news programs that start off saying hey folks, everything's great today.

Why? Man bites dog draws a lot more people than anything else. If it's a negative thing, then the news wants it. We get bombarded by negative messages every day. It's a wonder that people are as positive as they are sometimes.

Paul's question is this: "When things seem to be going wrong inside, such as negative emotions, how do you personally deal with these rather than burden others with your woes?" That's a tough one, really hard. Sometimes it helps to have someone else to talk to, a good friend, a spouse, or confident. It is hard to separate personal from professional.

I always like to say your life is your business, and your business is your life, or your job is your life, and your life is your job. People always say to leave your problems at home. That's easy to say to people, but it's harder to do. There's a similar problem in baseball. If a baseball player is in a terrible hitting slump, it usually affects his fielding and his defense.

It's easy to say leave your hitting problems in the dug-out; don't take them out on the field with you, but the problem is that we're human. We're not robots, and so it helps to have someone to talk it out with. It's not an easy solution, Paul, but if you have a good friend, a confidant, or a spouse that you can talk these problems over with, that is the way to discuss your problems.

Your business acquaintances and most of the people in your life really don't want to hear your problems. Why? They have problems of their own. It might be tough to hear it, but you really have to give a good face to the outside world. I think through the problems and I like to look for silver linings in everything. I really believe that things happen for a reason, and everything bad that happens to us we can turn into a good thing. I see that in all walks of life. Every time something bad happens, it can become a good thing.

I'll never forget what happened to me. I had the opportunity to speak for the Million Dollar Roundtable, which is a huge organization in the life insurance industry and a very prestigious platform. I had only been speaking for three, four years at the time, it was a tremendous opportunity and I remember getting there and being very excited.

I ran downstairs to register and get my program. I opened up the program and every speaker's picture is in the program. They have some of the best speakers in the world. Right above my name, there's a blank space. My picture was not in there. I'm saying to myself, "Well, people are going to think this moron didn't send his picture in. He's the only one stupid enough."

They had lost my picture and never told me. Then I see they put the wrong description of my session in there. They put a description that was a very product-oriented, bland, boring sounding session. So, first off, no one knows who I am because my picture is not in the program. Second of all, they're going to look at the session and say, "Wow, this session is boring. Why go there? Besides, this guy didn't even send his picture in." So I'm thinking all these things.

I decided not to complain. Let's make the best out of it. The only thing you can do at this point is give the best speech you can possibly do and give the audience what they came for. I got up there, and I turned it around. Basically I said, "You know, you're going to remember me more than you're going to remember anybody else here." I said, "You know why? Because every single speaker—you're never going to say to yourself, I saw a great speaker at Million Dollar Roundtable. I can't remember his name, but you know him. He's the guy whose picture *was* in the program."

But you could say, "You know, there was a guy at Million Dollar Roundtable. This guy was really great. You remember him. He's the guy whose picture was *not* in the program." Yes, Warren Greshes, that's me. I remember after this was all done, people were yelling and screaming and cheering. At the cocktail party that night, they said, "Oh, I heard about you. You're the guy whose picture was not in the program." Yes, that's me.

People started calling me up after the conference was done from all over the world, asking me to speak at their conferences and conventions because they'd all heard about the guy whose picture was not in the program. I think one of the keys to all these negative emotions and negative things is always look for the silver lining in that.

My son went through something tough when he was in high school. He played on the high school baseball team, and was practicing and working so hard to get better and better, all summer. I must have hit this kid thousands and thousands of ground balls and thrown thousands of pitches to him in the batting cage.

He worked out with a trainer and other coaches, and he was so ready for the season. During the first game, he played like a champion, and in the second game, he hurt his back, stress fracture. He missed the entire season.

Sometimes you get to appreciate something more when you don't have it, and I think that's what happened with Michael. He just worked hard. He's worked hard all summer. He didn't play ball, but he worked with a trainer and worked out harder and harder to strengthen the muscles in his back. Then he went back to the team and appreciated it even more. He even worked harder at school because he had learned about falling down rather than failing.

He learned that he didn't fail. He just fell down, and he got back up again. I'm real proud of him for not only playing ball again, but starting on the varsity team as a junior.

Negative things are going to happen to all of us, and we're all going to have problems. It's not what happens to you that matters, it's what you do about it.

Customer Service Diary

Today's story is great one. It comes from Jamie, out in Colorado. Jamie said, "Here's another worst customer service experience. A company left their business card on my front door, advertising their lawn services. Their services seemed interesting, and what made the deal seem even better was that underneath the telephone number was this, 'To make an appointment, call us 24 hours a day, 7 days a week.'

I kept the card for a couple of days and one evening decided to make an appointment. The call was answered by a voicemail menu that went on through at least through six or seven layers of choices." I'm sure most of you folks are familiar with that.

"If you have called for Roy, press one; for Jim, press two, etc. If you are a current customer, press one, new customer, press two, etc. Please choose from the following services that you are inquiring about. For aeration, press one; for sprinkler repair, press two, etc., and so forth. Finally, after working my way through this menu, a man's voice said, 'You have called after hours. Please hang up and try during our regular business hours.' Click."

Can you believe that? The whole purpose of this was 24 hours a day, 7 days a week. It's unbelievable. There are so many people out there who have no idea about how to do business. Let's talk about the whole concept of promising more and delivering less. I don't think there is anything that is more damaging to a business than making a bold promise such as call 24/7, getting people all excited, and then not backing it up.

I think it's exactly the opposite—promise less, deliver more.

I get some amazing stories in this customer service corner. Here is a beautiful one. It's just incredible to me how few people that do home repairs or lawn service really understand how to do business. Usually it is just a matter of following up, returning a phone call, showing up on time. It is so easy to differentiate yourself from the competition. All you've got to do in most cases is just call back.

I had one of my agents call me the other day, and she said, "We have a client that's very serious about booking you to keynote one of their conventions, and they'd like to know if you would call them up and talk to them first. They want to talk to you and make sure that you're the right person and whatnot." I said, "Great. I'd love to."

In fact, I ask my agents to please let me do that because I know if I can get them on the phone I can close the deal 99 times out of 100. Well, I got the client on the phone, and a half hour later, it was a done deal, and I'll be speaking at their convention in January. I'm thrilled about it. It's a wonderful client.

When I called the agent back with the news she said, "You mean it? You closed the deal?" I said, "Yes, it's done." And "Please, if you ever get anybody who is interested, let me know." She said, "You know, we had another speaker that they were also considering, but when I asked him if he would call the client, he said no. He couldn't understand why he would have to do that and why the client would want to talk to him."

That just blew me away, that someone would even think like that. If a prospective client wants to talk to you, then why wouldn't you pick up the phone and do it? If you're not willing to talk to somebody to get their money, what makes the client think you're going to talk to them after you've got their money? I'm always worried about that. If I get bad service from somebody who hasn't even gotten my money yet, then forget it. I know it's just going to be a nightmare once they have my money.

I hope by now you are ready to bust through your own self-imposed limitations, and remember, it's okay to be afraid, but it's not okay to let the fear stop you.

Setting Goals

This is something that so few people do, yet those who do it end up being so much more successful than their competition. Get ready to find out the three reasons why you should write down your goals, the most indisputable analogy you've ever heard for why goals need to be written, and the three components of an effective written goal. Read, listen, learn, and most of all, do something about it.

It's always time to set some goals and create a focus and direction in your life, career, or business.

I'm sure you know that people start making resolutions when it's coming up to another New Year. I've got to tell you, as you must know; most New Year's resolutions are garbage. Ninety-nine percent of them are going to end up dead by the time February or March rolls around.

If you belong to a health club, exercise or work out regularly, did you ever notice how health clubs always oversell their memberships? Do you know why? Very simply, because they know most people are never going to show up. Because most people make New Year's resolutions that they're going to get into shape, and they never show up.

When is a health club the busiest? Health clubs are the busiest in January when you've got all the New Year's resolution people trying to get in shape come heck or high water, and somewhere around March, you can pretty much exercise by yourself.

It might get busy again around May or June because we're running into bathing suit season, but the rest of the year, forget it. It's empty because people don't set a goal; they just make a statement. A New Year's resolution is just a statement—I want to lose weight, I want to get in shape, I want to quit smoking—but they never really sit down and plan it out. They never set a goal. They never develop a plan. They never write it down, and that's what we're going to talk about today. We're going to talk about the difference between goals and dreams and resolutions.

First and foremost, we're going to talk about goals. We're going to talk about setting goals and why you should write down your goals. I am also going to show you why. I'm going to show you why in such a way that's going to be so relevant to your everyday life and so easy for you to understand that there's going to be no way that you can possibly dispute me. Then after I've told you why and shown you why, I'm going to show you how. We're going to actually cover the three most important components of a very good, solid, focused, written goal.

Let's start off by talking about goals and why you should write down your goals. There are three very good reasons why you should be writing down your goals.

I'm going to start the first one off with a question, and the question is this: Have any of you ever woken up in the middle of the night with a good idea? I'm sure you have.

Now, when you woke up in the middle of the night with a good idea, what do you usually do? You probably went back to sleep, right? You went back to sleep.

Maybe you woke up at 3:00 in the morning with that great idea, you got very excited about it, you went back to sleep, and you woke up a few hours later, maybe 7:00 in the morning, what happened? Gone! You forgot it.

On the other hand, did you ever wake up in the middle of the night with a good idea and write it down? And then what happened? You went back to sleep, you woke up a few hours later, you took a look at that pad next to your bed, you looked at that good idea you wrote down, and what happened? You got real excited about it. So, the single biggest reason, one of the single biggest reasons, I should say, to write down your goals comes right under the heading of things that sound dumb but are true, and that says you write down your goals so that you don't forget them.

There are always people who dispute me on this, who say, "Well, I don't have to write down my goals. I mean, my goals, those are things that are really important to me. Those are some of the biggest things in my life, and if they're that important to me, I'm not going to write them down." Well, yes, I guess you're right to a degree.

Remember that great idea you woke up with about 3:00 in the morning? That was really important to you too. That was so important it woke you up at 3:00 in the morning, and you got so excited about that great idea. And four hours later that great idea that was going to make you millions—gone. You forgot it.

So, the question is how long until you forget your goals, the most important things in your life? Maybe 8 hours? Maybe 16? Maybe 24, 48? The first reason to write down your goals is very simply so that you don't forget them.

The second reason is that the writing down of a goal is the first commitment to actually doing it, to actually going out and doing it, to getting that goal, to achieving it. I know as well as you do that you all have goals. You have dreams. We all do. But you know that big stuff? I mean the really big stuff that you want. I mean the really important stuff. That's the kind of stuff that could take you two, three, five, ten years of time, energy, effort, and hard work to achieve.

Let me ask you, if you're not willing to take five or ten minutes to write it down, I mean, what makes you think that you're going to be willing to take two, three, five, ten years of hard work, energy, and effort to going out and getting it? So, the writing down of the goal is a commitment. It's the first commitment to actually going out and doing it.

The third reason to write down your goal has to do with accountability. In other words, the writing down of a goal makes you responsible, makes you accountable to the one and only person that you cannot fool, and that's you. If we really want to tell the truth about it, we can fool anyone we choose. We can fool our spouse. We can fool our kids. We can fool our friends. We can fool our coworkers. We can fool our boss. We can fool the people that report to us. We can fool anyone we choose. There's always one person though who knows the absolute God's honest truth at all times, and that's us.

I don't think you're going to want to look yourself in the mirror every morning if you're not willing to go after what you claim you really want out of life. You see, when we write down that goal, we're making ourselves accountable. Once we do that, once we write down that goal, it's very hard to not want to give it our best shot to at least try to go after what we say we really want out of life. Once you write it down, it's almost a contract with yourself, and you really don't want to admit to yourself that you weren't willing to do what it takes.

Now, there are some people, there are many people out there who, well, they figure if they don't write down their goals, then they don't have to be accountable, then they don't have to admit that they weren't willing to do it. Out of sight, out of mind. But even if you don't write it down, you still have to look in the mirror every morning and admit to yourself that you just weren't willing to do it.

To repeat and review, the three reasons why you should be writing down your goals, very simply is (a) so you don't forget them; (b) because it's the first commitment to actually doing it; and (c) it makes you accountable to the one and only person that you cannot fool, and that is you.

I said I was going to tell you why you should write down your goals, but now I'm going to take this a step further. I'm going to show you why. And once I show you why it should be very easy for you to understand and should be even easier for you to relate to.

Think about this question. Have you ever done the grocery shopping? I'm talking about real grocery shopping. I don't mean all you single guys out there with a jar of mayonnaise and a six pack. You know it's true. If you look in any single guy's refrigerator, all you usually see is a jar of mayonnaise and a six pack.

I always know what the six pack is for, but I could never figure out why the mayonnaise? They always tell you the same thing, "Well, it's for sandwiches," but they never have any bread or any meat. It's as if they live in hope that someone will show up with bread and meat so they can have sandwiches before the mayonnaise turns green.

For those of you that do real food shopping think about this. Think about going shopping with a written list. I also want you to think about going shopping without a list. Now, if you've done that, tell me, what's the difference?

You know as well as I do what the difference is. Whenever you've gone without a list, you usually end up buying more stuff. You buy a lot of stuff you didn't need. You probably spend more money when you go without a list. You probably spend a lot more time without a list, and I'll bet you forgot a lot of things that you wanted to buy when you went without the list.

Basically, what I find with every group I ask this of, they always say we buy more stuff. We buy stuff we didn't need. We forget stuff we needed. We spend more money. We spend more time. Basically what most people are telling me when I pose this question to them is they're saying that when they go out there without a written, focused direction or a plan, what happens is they end up wasting time, wasting money, taking on a lot of things that they did not need, and forgetting a lot of things that they did need. By the way, did I mention anything about food shopping in that last statement? No. That could apply to your life.

Okay, now think about this. You go food shopping. You go with a written list. Did you ever notice that when you go with a list how the shopping just seems to flow? You just go aisle by aisle, and it just seems to move.

Have you ever made a shopping list by aisle? My wife can do that, and I know quite a few people that can do it. They can make up a shopping list by aisle. While some of you might laugh at that, I will tell you that people that can make up a shopping list by aisle usually get their food shopping done faster than the rest of us. Why? Because they've already done the food shopping in their minds before they've ever gotten to the store.

In other words, in order to make up a shopping list by aisle, you first have to visualize. When you're making up a shopping list by aisle, you're literally visualizing yourself going up and down those aisles and buying whatever you need. It's what I call seeing yourself successful. You're creating a picture in your mind of what you really want, and you're going up and down those aisles. So, by the time you've got there, you've done that food shopping in your mind.

But now you ever notice how it just seems to flow when you go with a list? But now think about what happens whenever you go food shopping without a list, right? You always seem to be running from one end of the store to the other. You go to one end of the store, you grab from a shelf, "Oh, geez, I forgot something at the other end of the store." So, you've got to run all the way to the other end of the store. You grab something off the shelf, and you go, "Oh my God. I've got to go back to the other end of the store."

And you can't say I'll wait until later to go back to get the thing you forgot on the other end of the store because you don't have the list. If it's not written down, you're going to forget it anyhow. You're going to leave without it. So, you say to yourself, "Oh my God, what am I going to do?" So, you go to the other end of the store. You're running back and forth.

Did you ever do this? Did you ever have a conversation with the peanut butter shelf? You know what I'm talking about. You stand in front of that peanut butter shelf, and you say, "Do we have that? Now, I'm sure we have a jar at home. I'm sure the kids told me there's a jar in the cabinet over above the stove. No, I can swear we ran out of that. I'm wondering, I think in the other cabinet, there might be a jar there."

People are going walking by, and they're saying to themselves, "My God, why is this nut talking to the peanut butter shelf?" And you're standing there, and all of a sudden you say, "Oh, what the heck?" You grab another jar. You get home, what do you find? Three jars, three jars from the other three conversations you had with the peanut butter shelf.

We're going to look at when you go with a list and when you go without a list. When you go with a list, how long does it usually take you? How long does it usually take you to put together that shopping list, to actually write down your shopping list? What do you think, five minutes? Ten minutes? I'd say in most cases most people usually tell me anywhere from five to ten minutes.

Now, how long does it take you to actually do the food shopping? I don't just mean going and buying the food. You have to get in your car and drive to the store. You get to the store; you have to go up and down the aisles, putting the food in the baskets. You get on the checkout line. You have to get it all bagged. You have to load up the car again and drive back home. You unload the car. You have to put everything away. How long does that entire process take? I'd say probably about an hour and a half to two hours mostly to get that whole process done.

Now, let's look at going without a list. I want you to think about this. When you go food shopping without a list, how much time do you think you really waste? Most people usually say about half an hour. I'd say about half an hour, 45 minutes even.

Here's the big question, how much extra money do you think you blow, you just throw away when you go without a list? Let's say you spend an extra $40 when you're going without that list.

So, what we're saying is this. The willingness to take that ten minutes up front to put together a written, focused direction and plan for something as unimportant as food shopping, within an hour and a half to two hours has saved you 30 minutes in time. Remember the time you'd waste if you didn't have the list. That's a 300% return on investment and time, and put an extra $40 in your pocket, in something totally unimportant.

That's what planning is. Planning is a willingness to stop. It's a willingness to take a step back, to sit down and say, "I've got to stop and create a single focused direction for myself." We all know those people who are so busy; they don't have time to do this? They're so busy. They've got to go, they got to do it. They don't have time. I can't do this, the kind of people that can't even make a lunch appointment with you, the kind of people that carry around a 200-pound day timer, the kind of day timer that you need to take a seminar to learn how to use. They can't have lunch with you. They can't make an appointment because they don't know how to use the book. They're so busy.

You know what I call those people? Human gerbils. We all know what a gerbil is. It's a hamster-type animal. Gerbils have the cage. Gerbils have the wheel. The gerbil is without a doubt the busiest little sucker in the entire world because he gets on that wheel, and he just goes.

But you know something else about the gerbil? He never gets anywhere. He never gets off the wheel, and that's what human gerbils are like. And that's what planning is, it's the willingness to take a step back. It's the willingness to say, "Hey, stop!"

I can't run off in every single direction and not know where I'm going. It's like being Alice in Wonderland when she asked the Cheshire Cat, "There's all these different roads here. Which one do I take?" He said, "Where are you going?" She said, "I don't know." He said, "Well, in that case, any one's fine." So, it's the willingness to take that step back. Ten minutes to put together a written, focused direction and a plan, within an hour and a half to two hours got you back a 300% return on investment in time and put another $40 in your pocket in something as unimportant and irrelevant as food shopping.

Could you imagine what kind of return on investments you could get if you would do something like that for your life and your career? That's why you write down your goals.

Be Effective—
Write It Down

I told you how. I showed you how. I told you why. I showed you why. You have no excuse. Next we're going to talk about what goes into writing down an effective written goal. There are three components of an effective written goal.

The first component of an effective written goal is that you must be specific. Most people have what I call very vague goals. They talk in terms of I want more, I want better. In other words, I'd like to have a better job. I'd like to make more money. I want to make a lot of money. I'd like to have a nicer house. What does that really mean? What is a lot of money? What does nicer mean? What does more mean? And that's what I want to explore with you today. What does all of this mean?

The problem with saying things like more and a lot is that you are not defining them. How do you go after that sort of stuff? In other words, everybody's "a lot" is different. What's a lot to one person is not a lot to another person. A lot to me is not necessarily a lot to you. If we don't know how to define a lot, how do we know what we have to do to get it? And how do we know that we didn't already have it but because we couldn't find it, we didn't write it down, it just kind of passed us by?

To repeat: the first component of an effective written goal is to be specific.

I don't want people talking about things like more, better, got to do better in school, got to do better at work, got to have a bigger house. It doesn't mean anything. Many of you are salespeople. How many sales do you have to make to make a lot of money? A lot, right? A lot. Now, how many people do you have to see to make a lot of sales to make a lot of money? A heck of a lot. Now, how many people do you have to call to see a lot of people to make a lot of sales to make a lot of money? A heck of a lot more than that.

How do you know when to stop? And don't tell me you don't stop. Everybody says that, "Oh, we don't stop." Yes, you stop. You stop every day. If you don't know what a lot is, how do you know you didn't stop short?

Did you ever have one of those days when the first three people you called say, "Drop dead"? You say, "Okay, that's a lot." Well, how do you know you didn't have to speak to five people that day? You know why? Because you don't know what "a lot" is for you. If you don't know what "a lot" is for you how do you know what you have to do to get it? How can you formulate a plan to get it, and if you don't know what it is how do you know you didn't already have it but because you couldn't recognize it, because you couldn't define it, you just kind of let it pass you by?

Be specific. I'll never forget many years ago I was doing a seminar in New York City and I asked the audience to give me the definition of success. I got what I call the usual suspects—fame, power, recognition, money.

To the guy who said money, I said, "What'd you mean by that? Did you mean a lot of money?" He said, "Oh, yes, a lot of money." I said, "Well, what's a lot of money?" He said, "Whatever will make me comfortable." I said, "What will make you comfortable?" He said, "Whatever will get me everything I want." I said, "What do you want?" He said, "A lot of money."

I've got to tell you we went around in this circle for what seemed like forever. Finally, I said, "Give me a number. What's a lot?" He said, "$80 billion." Now, I had to admit, that's a lot of money, but I want you to see what happened next. I said to him, "Okay, you got it. You got the $80 billion. What are you going to do with it?"

If you don't know what you're going to do with it, what's the motivation to get it? Why do you think most lottery winners go broke? People say, "Well, if I win the lottery, I'm going to pay off my debts." What, you've got $50 million in debt? "If I win the lottery, I'm going to buy a house." You really need to win the lottery to buy a house?

So, I said, "What are you going to do with it?" He said, "I'm going to spend it." I said, "What are you going to spend it on?" He said, "I'm going to buy everything." I'm trying to figure out how do you do that? How do you buy everything?

I said, "What are you going to do, just back a truck up to Macy's and say give me everything?" He said, "No, you don't understand. I'm going to buy the United States." I said, "Stop. Stop right there." I said, "Could you buy the United States for $80 billion?" He said, "No." I said, "Well, then, is that a lot of money?" He said, "I guess not."

You see, it's only a lot if it's going to get you what you want, but if you don't know what you want, how do you know what you have to do to get it? Like I said, if you don't know what it is, how do you know you didn't already have it but because you couldn't define it, you just kind of let it pass you by? So, be specific.

The second component of an effective written goal is to make a timeframe. When you write down a goal I want you to write down the date or the year you intend to achieve it by. Why? If you don't have that, it's not a goal. It's a dream. A goal is a dream with a deadline.

I hear a lot of people say, "Well, I'm going to start my own business." "When?" "Oh, sometime. Don't worry; I'm going to do it sometime." I had a friend like that. He was going to do all the great things in the world, but he was going to do them all sometime. You can imagine how many of them he did. How about zero? Well, I'm going to get around to that sometime.

The word sometime is a very interesting word. You know what I love about the word sometime? The word sometime has the word "time" in it, but we know it really means never. I want you to think about this. Think about how we use this word, "sometime." For instance, any of you with kids, have you ever asked them to do something around the house, and they say, "Don't worry, Mom, don't worry, Dad"? "When are they going to do it?" "I'm going to do it sometime." Right?

Now, when they say that, what do you know? You know it's never going to get done. "When are you going to do your homework?" "Oh, sometime." "When are you going to take out the garbage?" "Oh sometime." It's never going to get done.

Here's another example. Let's say you want to sell me something. You call and say, "Warren, I want to come over and see you. I want to come over and see you sometime." I say, "Yes," and hang up. When are you going to come over? Well, you better come over right away because other than that, you never know when I'm going to be here.

Here's another scenario for you. You're walking down the street, and you see someone approaching you. You don't really dislike them; you don't really like them. You don't care if you see this person again, but you're stuck. You can't get away. It's too late. They've seen you. You can't cross over to the other side of the street, so you have one of these great conversations.

They go like this: "Hey, you look fantastic; haven't seen you in ages. You look great; we should get together sometime. Better yet, I'll give you my number. Give me a call sometime." I'll call you—sometime.

Why do you say that? You say that because you don't care about seeing that person again. So, what are we saying? We use this word, "sometimes" when we don't want to do something. What are we saying when we take this word, "sometimes" and put it on the end of our goals, our dreams, and our aspirations? We're saying they're never getting done.

The third component of an effective written goal is to place no limits on your ability to achieve. If it's what you really want, write it down. Write it down. Be specific, set a timeframe and don't ever place any glass ceilings over your head.

Once you say something like, "This is what I really want, but I don't think I can get it, so I will settle for this." The second you say, "I will settle for," that's as far as you are going, because you are already convinced you're never going to get any further. It's a self-fulfilling prophecy.

I hate when people say set realistic goals. I cringe when I hear that. Because when people say, set realistic goals, that's code. The word "realistic" is a code word. It really means low. What they're saying is set your goals so low that you cannot fail. Remember we talked about the difference between falling down and failing. Set your goals so low that you cannot fail. What are you looking to do here? Are you looking to not fail, or are you looking to succeed?

Don't worry about reality. Reality will set in. When? Reality will set in when you get to the planning stage. What determines whether a goal is realistic or not is you. When you get to the planning stage and you have to decide whether you are willing to do what it takes to achieve this goal, then it becomes realistic or it doesn't.

Someone once said to me, "You said there's no such thing as realistic goals. You don't like them? Okay. Next year, I'll tell you what, I want to make $10 million." You know what I said? "So, who's stopping you?" Lots of people in this country have made $10 million in a year. That's the beauty of America.

But watch what happened. I said to him, "I'm going to tell you what you've got to do to make that $10 million." I went through a whole list on what he had to do to make that $10 million. I got to the bottom of the list, he said, "Whoa, that's not realistic." I said, "It's not the goal that's not realistic; it's that you are not willing to do what it takes to achieve that goal."

What's realistic? If a young girl comes up to you, she's eight, nine years old, and she says to you, "Someday I want to be an Olympic figure-skating champion," are you going to tell her that's not realistic? Of course it's realistic. People do it. It's been done. It's hard. Of course it's hard. It has to be hard, because if it was easy, everyone would do it. It's hard. She's going to have to sacrifice. She's going to have to sacrifice for years and years and years. She's going to have to sacrifice starting at that young age in order to achieve that. It's hard.

Not a lot of people make it, but it is realistic. If you're willing to do what it takes, it's realistic. If you're not willing to sacrifice and do what it takes, then it's not realistic. What determines whether a goal is realistic or not is you. Are you willing to do what it takes to achieve that goal?

I love talking about goals. There was a study done at Harvard University regarding goals. They surveyed a graduating class and found that only 3% of them had written goals. They also found that 20 years later, that 3% had accumulated more wealth than the other 97% combined.

We can see there the value of having goals and writing them down. Write down your goals and write effective goals. The three components of effective goals are to be specific, use timeframes, and place no limits on your ability to achieve. That's how you write down your goals and ensure your goals are effective.

Your Personal Action Plan

Now it's time to take your dreams and goals and learn about forming them into an action plan. So, read, learn, and most of all, do something about it.

Now that you've got your goals written down, and hopefully you do, and if not, it's the time to do it. It's always the time to do it. To review: you have goals. They're specific. They have a timeframe on them. In other words, when you write down a goal, you should write down the year you intend to achieve it by. And please remember, with your goals; place no limits on your ability to achieve. If it's what you really want, write it down.

Now that you've got your goals, now we've got to start planning, but before we do, here's an email from James in Waterloo, Ontario. He asks, "When writing down your goals, lifetime goals, three-to-five-year goals, daily goals, how many goals are reasonable, and how long should you take to write up your list?" And then he asks, "What about accomplishment review? Is there any methodology one should follow or should you just stroke off the tasks on your list and forget them?"

Those are great questions, and let's take them one at a time. The first question was how many goals are reasonable and how long should you take to write up your list? My feeling is this, if you're not used to setting goals, if it's something you haven't done before, then I would put down three goals, three of each category, and the categories are short-term goals, anything up to a year; intermediate goals, two to three years; and long-term goals, five to ten years.

I would do no more than three of each category, and I say this is because if you haven't done this before, then you don't want to bite off more than you can chew. I want you to enjoy this. I want you to see the benefit of it. I want you do to it all the time, and I know if it's too hard for you to implement at the beginning, then you're going to give up, and you're not going to do it anymore.

So, start off with three. For those of you that have done this before, hey, write as many as you want. As many goals as you want, that's fine by me, but for those of you that haven't done this before, three short-term goals, three intermediate goals, three long-term goals.

Now, what about accomplishment review? Obviously, for your daily goals just cross them off. That feels great. But on the other goals, the one-year goals, two-, three-year, five-, and ten-year goals, I like to sit down and review my goals every three months, I mean, really look them over, and the biggest reason why is because priorities change. What's important to us today might not be important to us three months from now.

You know, when you're young and single, you want to buy a fancy nice red Porsche or some kind of sports car. All of a sudden, you get married, and six months later, it's SUV time, and the sports car is not that important. So, sit down, review your goals. Make sure that what you wrote down is still what you really want. I think that's the biggest reason to review them.

By the way, once you've accomplished a goal, cross it off, set another one. Those of you with only three goals, once you do one, set another one. Keep churning in the goals. Get used to it. Get in the habit of setting goals. Every three months, review your goals, see that they're still important to you. Those that aren't import-ant to you anymore, get rid of them. It's okay. It's yours. The goal-setting police aren't going to kick down your door and say, "Hey, pal, come with me." It's all right. So, that would be my answer to the question for James.

Let's talk about planning.

The plan is the key. Everyone who has ever been successful has a plan. I'm talking about a written action plan. I'm talking taking your goals and formulating a plan to achieve each and every one of them. The plan is the magic formula. It is the magic formula that answers the question that I hear so often from people, "How do I keep the motivation going?" I get excited about my goals. I get excited about when I first do them, but how do I keep it going once I start?

How do I keep the motivation going? What do I do to stay excited once I get my goals?"

I get these goals, I write them down, I get excited, I start out after them, but then after a couple weeks or a month or so, I'm just not as excited anymore. That's why you need the plan, because the plan is what keeps you excited. The plan, a written plan, is like the roadmap. Basically, the written plan is taking the big goal and breaking it down into smaller, easier-to-accomplish goals. That's how it keeps you going.

The problem is this; when you have a goal and you don't have a plan, you give yourself no roadmap. You give yourself no stopping off point. You give yourself no accomplishment stops, as I like to call them.

Let's take, for example, a person with a goal but no plan. Let's say your goal, it doesn't even matter what it is, a year down the road, two years down the road, three, five years down the road. The problem you have is that when you don't have a plan, all you're giving yourself is an end result. You see, just by setting a goal, you've just given yourself a destination. You said this is where I want to end up. This is when I want to get there by. The plan is what says these are the actual steps I will take to get there.

Now, you wake up in the morning without a plan, but you have a goal. The problem is the only thing you have to focus on is that end result, is that goal. Every day you wake up, that's all you're looking at. That's all you see, is that end result, is that goal. Now, that goal could be a year away, two years away, five years away, but every day you're looking up, and you're seeing that goal, and you're not there yet. It doesn't matter how long it's supposed to take, all you're giving yourself to focus on every day is the goal, the timeframe and the fact that you're not there yet. Sooner or later, how are you going to feel?

You're going to start to feel frustrated. That's right. And if you keep feeling frustrated, the more frustrated you feel, what are you eventually going to do? You're going to give up. As you know, I believe the only time you ever fail is when you give up.

Now, watch what happens when you have the plan. You take a plan and you put down your stopping off points, each step of the plan. Now, when you get up in the morning, you no longer have to focus on the end result, on the goal. All you need to focus on is the next step, and the next step is closer. The next step is easier to accomplish. You wake up. You go after it. You do it. You accomplish it, and how do you feel? You feel great. That's right. You feel great. You feel energized. And because you feel great, what are you going to do? You're going to take the next step. That's right.

You see, the beauty of the plan is it gives you the ability to give yourself the motivation to keep going, to take that next step. What can I do for myself to take that next step, to keep myself going? That's why you need the plan, because the plan is those stopping off points. So, now I'm ready to take that next step. Now the only thing I need to focus on is not the end result; it's just the next step.

The only time I ever need to focus on the end result is when the end result becomes the next step, and then it's closer. It's there. I can get it. As I keep accomplishing each one of these steps, imagine the kind of confidence that builds within you. Imagine how you start to feel. You start to feel invincible as if nobody can stop you.

That's the beauty of the plan. The real fun in life is not in the being there. The real fun in life is in the getting there. As anybody who's ever done it before knows, the fun is always in the fight. The fun is not in the end result. If you think of all the great things you've ever accomplished in your life, we always look back on what it took to get there. That's what we always talk about. Those are the stories we always tell. Those are the things we always embellish, we lie about to our friends is all the great things we did to get there, not in the finally being there. Once you're there, it's on to the next thing.

The Three Components
of an Effective Plan

The plan is going to keep you motivated. The plan is going to keep you excited. The plan is what is going to keep you going every single day.

How do you formulate the plan? There are three components that go into a truly effective plan. An effective plan is expressed in continuous action. An effective plan is broken down into accomplishable steps, and an effective plan gives you the ability to measure your progress every step of the way.

These are all key components in an effective plan. For any goal you have, you're going to have an effective plan to achieve them as long as you have these three components in your plans.

Let's look at the first component which is that an effective plan is expressed in continuous action. It is very important to be able to take a goal and to break it down into its smallest pieces. In other words, if I know what I have to do every day, every week, every month, every year in order to get to the goal, if I can break it down in a total continuous action, literally telling myself if I do this, every day that I do "X," I get that much closer to my goal. Now, I'm more motivated.

Let me explain it further. Let's take salespeople. The average salesperson always works backward when they start their year. Their basic premise is well, if I make a lot of calls, I'm going to make a lot of money, except they never know what a lot is. You've had those days where the first three people you call say, "Drop dead," so you hang up the phone, and you say, "Okay, that's a lot."

But the problem is how do you know you should be speaking to five people that day? Because you don't know what a lot is. We've talked about a lot before when we talked about goal setting. You really need to be able to break it down. It's like losing weight—it's easier to lose a pound a month than twelve pounds in a year. It's easier to lose a half a pound a week than twenty-six pounds a year because we break it down into continuous action.

Let me show you what I'm talking about. A professional salesperson really understands what they need before the year starts. In other words, they formulate a plan that says first figure out the goal—the end result, the money—so we always start with the end result and we work backward. For any goal, start with your end result, and work backward.

So, the professional salesperson says, "Let me figure out how much money I need to make to support the lifestyle I choose to live in the next year." You figure out all your expenses, how much money you want to save, and what you're saving for. The goal for this year is also part of your long-term goals, so you need to think about how it ties in with that, vacations, supporting your family, putting money away for the kids for college, and saving for your retirement.

Now that I've got my number, I can formulate a sales plan to figure out what I have to do in order to achieve this ultimate goal. Now, let's take a nice round number, $100,000. Let's say that is the goal. A salesperson says I want to make $100,000 this year. That will give me the money I need to live the lifestyle I choose to live.

This is where planning and record keeping comes in, because the professional salesperson keeps good records. The professional salesperson might think, I've never made $100,000 in a year, so I really need to figure out how to do this. But from keeping records for the past year, I know that my average sale—I'm just using hypothetical numbers here—puts approximately $1,000 in my pocket.

Now I know I don't have to make $100,000. I have to make 100 sales. Making 100 sales is not the easiest thing in the world. Because I've never done it before, I have to formulate a plan. My plan is this: A hundred sales is hard, but you know what's easier? Two sales a week. Now I know I have to make two sales a week. It seems a lot easier to make two sales a week than it is to make 100 sales in a year.

Hold it a second—it's not always within my power to make those two sales. Sometimes people say no. Sometimes people say I've got to think about it, which is even worse than when people say no, because at least I they say no, I know to move on. So, now what do I do?

Now I've got to formulate a plan, but I know from keeping records that my closing ratio is one out of three. I know that I don't have to make two sales a week. I don't have to make $100,000 anymore. I don't have to make $2,000 a week. I don't even have to make two sales. I just have to see six people a week, because I know if I see six people a week that gives me my two sales on the average. That gives me my $2,000 in commission. That gives me $100,000 in a year.

But, you know, not everybody sees me. Some people won't see me. Some people I make appointments with don't show up. Some people don't show up, but I know from keeping records that most people do. In fact, I find that I hold about 25% of my appointments.

By the way the biggest reason that people don't show up for appointments is because salespeople bothered to call and confirm. You call up, "I just want to make sure that we're on today." And as soon as you say that, what are you telling the client? You're telling him he's got an out. If he doesn't feel like doing it, you've just told him it's okay.

So now you know on average you lose two appointments a week. I don't have to make any money anymore. I don't even have to sell this stuff. All I have to do is set up eight appointments a week. I set up eight appointments a week, I get to see six people, I get to close two sales, I get to make $2,000 in commission and $100,000

We're talking here about formulating your action plan. We're talking about expressing your plan in continuous action. I'm going through the process that a good professional salesperson goes through. We start off with the goal being $100,000 in income for the year, but then we break it down into how many sales we need. Because we're professional and we keep records, we figured out that breaks down into a hundred sales a year, or two sales a week.

Now, it's not always within your control to make two sales a week, but we know from your records because you're professional, that it takes three face-to-face presentations on the average to close one sale, so now we know you need to make six presentations a week to close the two sales to get the $2,000 to make the $100,000 a year. But now, like I said, it's not always within your control that people show up.

We know that 25% of the people cancel the appointments, so now we're at the point where we know we don't have to sell anything; we don't have to make any money. We just have to set up eight appointments a week. This job's getting easier, isn't it? But hold it a second. Not everybody gives you an appointment. Some people say, "Drop dead." Some people say, "I don't like your company." Some people say, "I've done business with you before. I had a bad experience." Sometimes you can't even speak to them because you can't get past the receptionist or you get the dreaded voicemail.

So, what do you do? Well, you know what? That doesn't happen on every call. Let's say because you keep good records, you know that one out of every five people you call gives you an appointment. One out of every five people you speak to, I should say. One out of every five people you speak to gives you an appointment.

I don't have to make any money. I don't have to sell any of this stuff, don't have to see these people. I don't even have to make any appointments. I just have to speak to forty people a week, because if I speak to forty people, one out of five gives me an appointment. That's eight appointments. I'll hold six of them. I'll close two of them, and I'll make my $2,000 a week, $100,000 a year.

But now, hold it a second. Like I said, not everybody speaks to me. Some people, I get the voicemail. Some people, I get the receptionist—could get a nine-year-old kid or an amazing dog barking. That doesn't always happen, because I know that. I keep records, and I know that one out of every three people I physically dial on the phone talks to me. I'm talking decision-makers. I'm not talking receptionists. I'm not talking assistant. I'm talking people that can make the decision. I know that one out of every three talk to me.

Now, hold it a second. I don't have to sell anything, don't have to make any money, don't have to set up appointments, and don't even have to speak to these people. I just need to physically dial the telephone 120 times a week or 24 times a day, because I know that if I dial that phone 24 times a day every single day, that's 120 dials a week. I'd speak to 40 people. I'd get eight appointments. I keep six of them. I close two. I make $2,000 on the average, put $100,000 in my pocket.

Now I know that every day I come to work, every single day I come to work and I make those 24 calls, I dial that phone 24 times, I'm getting that much closer to what I truly want, to my goal. Now, how motivated do you think that person is to prospect and to dial the phone? That's continuous action. What do I have to do on either a weekly or daily basis or even a monthly basis so that I keep going, so that I eventually get to my goal?

It's like working out. Instead of working out once every two weeks for two hours, you're better off working out three times a week for twenty minutes each time, because it's continuous action. By continuous action, you develop the habit. This is all about developing habits. That's what it's all about. You know, if you just exercise once a week or once every two weeks for two hours, do you really develop the habit? No. What happens? What happens is you start to dread exercise.

Let's say you haven't exercised in years, and for so many people this is true. Let's talk about health clubs in January, which is the month for health clubs. Health clubs know that their big business is in January because that's when all the New Year's resolution people come in. They come in, and they're going to get in shape in a week.

They come in, and exercise for two hours. Then next morning, they wake up and feel like a pretzel. Now what do they feel about exercise at this point? They hate it. They dread it. That's why they eventually all stop. That's why health clubs stop being busy by March, because people give up. But if you're working out just 20 minutes a day three times a week, you're doing it at your pace. Especially when you're starting off, you want to do it at the pace so you're not going to want to give up.

That brings me to the second step, which is to break down the goal into accomplishable steps. Formulate the plan. The second component of an effective written plan is to break it down into accomplishable steps. What does everybody always say? Standard motivational speaker 101, the toughest step of any journey is the first step.

We know that the toughest step to take is the first step. So why do so many people insist on making it the hardest one to accomplish? Why not make the first step the easiest to accomplish? We don't need to accomplish the plan on the first step. We just need that first step to get us going. That's the idea. As long as we get going, we have a shot to keep going.

So, why not make that first step easy and so easy to accomplish that we have no excuse not to do it? See, the purpose of the first step is to just get you to take it, because I know once you take that first step, you're going to accomplish it because it's so easy to accomplish. You're going to say hey, that wasn't so bad. Now I've got the incentive to take another step and another step and another step.

When you formulate the plan for any goal, make the first few steps, the first number of steps in that plan, very easy to accomplish, because what you're really trying to do is just get yourself going and develop the habit of accomplishment. You want to see some successes. What's wrong with helping to build yourself a winning streak? You know if you're on a winning streak you always feel more confident about what you're doing.

So, formulate the first steps. Make them so easy to accomplish that you have no excuse not to do it, and this way you'll be able to do it. You know, it's like exercising 20 minutes a day. Only do as much as you can do without wanting to quit. That's why I believe in activity goals. For salespeople, I like activity goals most of all, because activity, if done on a consistent, everyday basis, gets you sales. Activity is the key.

Now, if you have activity—people say to me, "If I make my 24 calls, if I have my activity goal and I'm on a roll, what should I do?" I said, "Stop." "Well, shouldn't I keep going?" No, don't keep going. Remember, first of all, what's wrong with stopping on a roll? What's wrong with stopping on a high note? Who knows? That next call could be that really bad one where the person tells you to drop dead because they don't want to talk to you anymore. They don't like salespeople. Why do you want to take that chance?

What's so bad about accomplishing your goal every single day? So, just do what you're capable of doing. Find your capability. Find your capability, then slowly increase it. In other words, if you know you need to make twenty calls a day, but right now you're only doing two or three calls a day, don't think you're going to go from two or three calls a day to twenty calls a day in one shot. It's not going to happen. It's like going from twenty minutes of exercise a day to two hours of exercise a day. It's just not going to happen. You're going to hate it so much that you're going to stop doing it.

I don't want you to stop, but let's say you're making two calls a day, and instead of making two calls a day from now on, you made three calls a day. Right away you increase your activity by 50%, and if you increase your activity by 50%, you can increase your sales by 50%.

Find your comfort level. You don't have to break out of your comfort level. You just have to go a little bit beyond it. But you've got to know where you are, so find your level and always look to go just a little bit beyond it. And do it on a gradual basis. Small changes implemented on an everyday basis will always yield you great results.

Let's talk about the third part of the planning process which is to give yourself the ability to measure progress every step of the way. Why do we need to be able to measure our progress? If we don't measure our progress, we'll have no idea that we made any. I'm wondering how many of you out there have given up on something because you felt you were making no progress when you really did make progress, and the only reason why you didn't know is because you couldn't measure it. Think about it.

Let's take a five-year goal an example. You have a five-year goal. Now, that five-year goal is sixty months away. If you start working towards that goal today, and you just make normal progress toward that goal, within three months, that's three months out of sixty, you should be 5% closer to that goal.

If you have no way of measuring this, if you do not give yourself the capability to measure this progress, would you really know you were 5% closer to that goal? And if you don't know it, what are you going to assume? What do most people assume? Most people assume the negative that they haven't made any progress at all. After all, you can't see, feel, or touch 5% progress in the air, so you're going to assume you made no progress at all.

You're going to assume you made no progress, and you're going to say to yourself, "You know, I've been working towards this goal every day for three months, and I feel as though I'm still on square one." The next thing out of your mouth is, "Why bother?" and you give up. You gave up on a goal that you were making progress on, but because you didn't give yourself the ability to see it, you just assumed it wasn't there. So, you've got to give yourself the ability to measure that progress.

Let me give you a great example. I'm going to take my two favorite salespeople, Salesperson A and Salesperson B. Okay, both of them have the same goal for the year. The goal is 144 sales. They want to close 144 sales by the end of the year.

Now, Salesperson B, he's a real smart guy. He says, "Well, I need to close 144 sales this year. That's no problem. I can do that. I don't need a plan. Why do you tell me plan? I don't need a plan. I'm a pro. I can do this. One hundred forty-four sales, I'm great. I'll do it."

Salesperson A, she was a little different. She said to herself, "Well, you know, I've never done this before, so I don't know if I can. So, I need to formulate a plan." What she found out was that she didn't have to make 144 sales in a year, she just had to make 12 sales a month. Okay, now, let's see what happens.

Salesperson A, she wakes up in the beginning of January, and she goes about her business. By the end of January, she has now closed 12 sales. Her goal for January was what? Twelve. She has closed 12 sales. What do you think she says to herself? Hey, right on target. How do you think she feels? She feels great. So, now what's her next goal? Her next goal is just 12, 12 for February.

Now, Salesperson B, he goes out beginning January and does the same thing as Salesperson A. He closes 12 sales in the month of January, but now what do you think he says to himself? "Oh my God, 132 to go. Oh, man!" What happens here is that people like Salesperson B don't maintain any control over their life or their career because they don't have a plan.

Somewhere around May 1st, I guarantee you Salesperson B is going to be saying to himself, "You know, I think this goal wasn't very realistic." Those of you who have heard me before know that I hate realistic goals, that they're just an excuse to set them low, that the only thing that's unrealistic is if you're not willing to do what it takes to achieve it.

You know that Salesperson B is one of these guys that always tells you what a great fourth quarter salesperson he is or what a great December salesperson he is because he didn't wake up until Thanksgiving to realize that he was in trouble. And Salesperson B is also one of these guys that totally loses control because what happens in

December if there's a freak snowstorm, and he can't get out and see people?

What happens if he gets the flu, and he can't get out for a day? What happens if his car breaks down, and he can't get out for a day? You know what happens? That one bad day starts to equal one bad year. And then you know what happens in January? In January, Salesperson B becomes one of these guys who could have bought a building 30 years ago for $9, you know, one of these excuse-makers, tells you all the things he could've done.

And he's going to say to you something like, "Hey, you know, I could've made quota. It's not my fault. How am I supposed to know that my car is going to break down? How am I supposed to know that I'm going to get sick? How am I supposed to know it's going to snow?"

He does have a point. He's can't know specifically that stuff was going to happen. But you know what he is supposed to know? He's supposed to know that something is going to happen, and you know why he's supposed to know that something's going to happen? Because you know as well as I do that it always does.

But now, let's look at Salesperson A. What if she gets the flu in December and she can't get out? What if her car breaks down, and she misses a day? What if there's a freak snowstorm, and she can't get out and sell for a day or two?

You know what her one bad day equals? Her one bad day equals one bad day. You know why? Because you see, the time to worry about December is not at the end of November. The time to worry about December is back in the first quarter of the year when you still have control. You see, Salesperson A has real control over her life and her career because she has planned.

Salesperson B, he's got no control, so he's going to blame everybody else for everything that's happened to him. That's why you need a plan. The plan must be expressed in continuous action. The plan must be broken down into accomplishable steps, and remember that the plan must always give you the ability to measure your progress every step of the way.

The next step is to take each goal that you've set and write each goal on a separate piece of paper. Write out the goal in full, and write down the year you intend to achieve it by. If you don't write down the year you intend to achieve it by, you don't have a timeframe, and if you don't have a timeframe, then it's not a goal, it's just a wish. You need a deadline. Write it down, and then list the steps that you will take to achieve each and every one of these steps under each goal.

Now what do you with your plan? I think you post it up somewhere where you can see it, somewhere you can see it every day. If you don't want other people to see it, post it inside your closet door. If you want other people to see it, that's fine. Remember, as I've told you with goals, other people can help you to achieve what you want, and that's great.

If you tell people what you're looking for, you never know where your next big break is coming from. So post it up where you can see it. You should be reviewing your goals and plans every three months, going over what you need, going over what's important to you, getting rid of what's not important to you.

What if you come to the deadline, and you haven't achieved your goal, what do you do? It's not the end of the world. You simply move back the deadline. This is yours, after all. You have formulated these goals and plans with a pen or a pencil on a piece of paper. You've typed it out. You have not taken a hammer and a chisel and chiseled them into a block of stone. They can change.

Your life will change. Your priorities will change. Don't worry about it. This is yours. You can do whatever you want with it, and the more you do with it, the more it's going to help you. The more you use it, the more it will help you. And remember, when you do achieve a goal, set another one. Constantly be setting challenges for yourself; constantly be looking to move forward.

Customer Service Diary

This is from Tywatha who writes, "Hi, Warren. The worst experience I can readily recall as a customer was when my husband and I went to purchase a computer. We had received ad after ad from this particular store. It seemed at the time to be the place to go get the computer. They were always running super deals. With all the options they offered, how could a person go wrong?

My husband and I entered the store with our three-year-old son in anticipation that we would leave with a computer. We walked around for what had to be at least 20, 30 minutes just looking before we were even approached by a salesman."

I would've been out of there by then. I'll tell you that.

"Finally, I asked for some help after being utterly frustrated because I did not know what I needed to meet my needs. The computer was going to be for home, work, and future educational needs, so of course I wanted something reasonable but within our needs as well. The sales manager I questioned stuck me with a trainee."

Tywatha, that was your next clue to get the heck out of there.

"The trainee had no clue what he was doing. First of all, he showed us the most expensive computer on the market which did not meet our needs at all. As a matter of fact, if we had purchased that computer, it would have made our lives even more hectic than now. I kept telling him what uses the computer would serve in our home. Those facts went in one ear and then out the other in a matter of seconds. Again, he showed a computer that did not meet out criteria.

Angry and frustrated, we left disappointed. Three nights later, we called the 800 number of Dell and spoke to someone who totally knew what we needed. We got a computer, CD burner, and three-in-one printer for a little over $800. The computer has software that is compatible with our home life as well as my work. If the salesperson had listened and had known his stuff about computers, he could've reaped the bonuses."

*   *   *

Thank you for your time, Tywatha. Now, I have to tell you, this is an all-too-familiar story. For those of you who insist on selling price, you might want to notice that in this case, price did the only thing it's really capable of doing, it got Tywatha and her family in the door. That's right; it got them in the door.

But once in the door, value takes over. You know, price might get us in the first time as customers, but price is not what keeps us coming back if we don't have good experiences. And Tywatha, obviously, had a terrible experience. This is where value takes over, and in this case, there was none.

The funny thing is Dell provided her the most value and a great price. If you can give a good price and great value, then the competition is in big trouble. They combined price, value, and ease. Think about this. Tywatha didn't even have to leave her house. That is an unbeatable combination.

Everybody wants a good price, but you know what most people do want? They want the value. I would pay a little bit more to get what I want. It's great to have a great price, but if it's not going to be what I want, then what the heck do I need your price for? I'm just going to have to buy something else, and then it's going to end up being even more expensive.

So, Tywatha got what she wanted without leaving the house, and price, once again, took a backseat. No doubt she would have bought from Dell even if it wasn't the cheapest price. Why? Because they gave her what she wanted.

What the 21st Century Customer Really Wants— Make My Life Easier

This chapter deals with two of the most pressing issues businesses are dealing with today: one, how do we differentiate ourselves from the competition, and two, how do we create and deliver the kind of value that makes us indispensable to our clients without having to sell price? This happens to so many salespeople and so many companies today.

We want to help you understand who the customers are and what they really want. We will explore such issues as how demographic changes in American society have changed who the customers are, what they buy, and why they buy, and why the internet is doing to salespeople what automation started doing to the factory floor over 20 years ago. So, listen, learn, and most of all, do something about it.

It's a tough issue. I don't know about you, but I find myself as a customer, and that's where I want to focus.

I am coming from the side of the customer and talking about what customers are looking for today. As a customer, I find myself buying a lot more online than I ever used to. I know everybody is. If you look at online sales, they're just climbing. One of the biggest reasons I buy online is so I don't have to deal with people. Isn't that terrible? But the fact of the matter is I've just gotten tired of dealing with people that I don't feel are professional enough for their job.

Isn't it terrible when you get more value dealing with a machine than you do dealing with a person? I very rarely walk into bookstores anymore. I just go right to Amazon.com, and I buy my books there. Not only do I get them cheaper, but I never have to leave my office. I don't have to pay sales tax, and sometimes if I buy enough books, I don't have to pay shipping either.

And you say well, you can sit in the bookstore and browse through the books, but you know what? You can now browse through books on Amazon.com. I just click on the books, and I'm browsing through books. Some books give you summaries. Some books give you sample chapters. I browse through the table of contents. It's easier than having to speak with people who many times don't know what the heck they're talking about.

For years, I've been buying my office supplies from a mail order company. I can buy them online. I can buy them through their catalog. I don't have to leave the office. My wife doesn't have to leave the office. We don't have to go to Staples and talk to somebody who's not familiar at all with what we're looking for.

It's amazing to me how many times I go into some of these places and can't find what I'm looking for. I watch the commercials telling me that they always have what I'm looking for, but they never seem to. So more and more, I find myself buying things online. I mean, I book all my air travel online now. I never talk to travel agents, never talk to anybody; I just book it right online.

The only airline I'll ever talk to usually is Southwest because they're the only ones that I find actually either give me answers or pick up the phone. I find the biggest reason people are buying online is because they can't find enough good people to buy from. So, we're going to talk about how do you become one of those good people?

One of the biggest problems today is that there are not enough people who understand that successful salespeople sell more than just the product or service. Successful companies sell more than just their product or service. Basically they understand what it is that they are really selling because they understand who the customer is and what they really want.

You know as well as I do that the world is changing. The business world of today, because of globalization, is probably more competitive than it's ever been in its entire history. There are companies out there that are monsters today that didn't even exist 20 or 30 years ago, companies like Microsoft, Intel—I mean monsters. Who were they?

Take a company like Walmart, who was Walmart 30 years ago? Thirty years ago Walmart was one man,

Sam Walton, putting up small stores in tiny backwoods towns where no other retailer wanted to be. In fact, when Sam Walton started, that was his marketing plan. His plan was to open stores in tiny towns where no other retailer wanted to be. Do you think that 30 years ago Sears considered Walmart competition? Probably not. Funny thing is 30 years later, you think Walmart considers Sears competition? Probably not.

So, what we're seeing here is that your competition can come from anywhere, can come from anytime, with globalization. Companies can pop up from all over the place. We are now competing with India. We're competing with China. We're competing with countries that we never thought we'd ever have to compete with. And as a customer, as a consumer, I can buy almost anything that I want over the internet, and I never have to talk to any of you.

So, the question now becomes, "What kind of extra value are you creating for all of your clients, customers, and prospects that makes it so much more beneficial for them to deal directly with you than to just click on their computers?" In other words, how are you differentiating yourself from the competition? If I was to ask you any one question today, it would probably be, "What are you really selling?" What are you *really* selling?

Are you just selling your basic product? Are you just selling your basic service? Are you just selling the first thing you pull out of your bag, or are you selling quality, extraordinary quality, service, convenience, and value? Are you selling things that save me time and make my life easier? Are you selling knowledge, expertise, information, and education, or are you just selling stuff?

Because if you are just selling stuff, if you are just selling what everyone else is selling, to be perfectly honest, I can just click on my computer, and I can buy stuff from the cheapest guy in town. In most cases I'll bet that's not you and that's not your company.

Let me help you understand what's going on in the marketplace. As a professional speaker, one of the big edges that I have over my clients is that I speak in all sorts of different industries. I speak to different companies, in all sorts of different marketplaces. That's one of the great things about my job, one of the things that I really enjoy more than anything is that I get to see what's going on in all these companies, industries, and marketplaces.

Let me tell you what I find is going on in every single company, in every single industry, in every single marketplace that I have walked into in probably the past five years, and it is this: The middle is dead. The middle is gone.

If you want to be successful in today's business world, in today's marketplace, you better be one of two things: either be the cheapest or the best, because the middle is gone. You see, you can no longer sell pretty good products or pretty good services at pretty good prices because I'll tell you something, pretty good is just not good enough anymore. I can buy pretty good products or pretty good services at dirt cheap prices now or I can buy better products or better services at just a little more expensive price. The middle is dead and gone.

You see it every day in your everyday life. Think about the stores that do business. Think about the stores that do not. On the one hand, you have your deep discounters, stores like Walmart and Target and Kohl's and others like that.

Even down at that end, I mean even down at that end where supposedly price is what drives every single sale, it's not just the price because if it was just the price that was driving all the sales, then how do we explain what happened to Kmart? Kmart's prices were pretty much similar to Walmart's or Target's or Kohl's. But they're pretty much gone. So, how do we explain that?

See, it's not just the price. Companies like Walmart aren't doing it on just the price because they give you a lot of other value. Everybody has gone to Walmart. I think if you live in America, you have to go to Walmart. You can't avoid it anymore. But if you ever go to Walmart, you notice a number of things about Walmart.

One thing I notice right away as soon as I walk into Walmart is how well-lit it is. It's incredible; you almost need sunglasses to shop in Walmart. To me, that's a great thing because I am what's called a lightbulb counter. Since I speak about this stuff, I'm checking everything, everywhere I go.

I always look up when I walk into a store. I want to see. When I talk about being a lightbulb counter, I want to see how many lightbulbs are out, because you know what that tells me about a company? What does that tells me about an organization when I look up and I see burned out lightbulbs, and no one is taking care of them? That tells me they don't care. And why do I know they don't care? Because changing a lightbulb, that's the easy stuff. And if they're not willing to do the easy stuff, right away I know they're not going to do the hard stuff.

I love Costco. I talk about it all the time. I think Costco is one of the greatest inventions of the 20th century. They're always running around changing lightbulbs in Costco. It is hard in those big warehouses with the high ceilings, but they're constantly changing the lightbulbs in Costco because Costco cares. They are not just the cheapest, they are the best. See, that's hard to beat when someone is both.

Walmart is always well lit. Walmart is well stocked. You can't go into Walmart and not find what you're looking for, and there are people at Walmart to help you, which is amazing to me. There are more people to help you at Walmart than in your average department store. So, you get all that stuff plus the prices.

Have you ever noticed what I call "holes" in the shelves? In retail terms, that means there's a lot of stuff missing. In today's society, where people are more rushed for time, where time is the most valuable commodity we have, no one wants to shop in a place where they might take a chance that that store might not have what they're looking for. People don't shop like that anymore. They don't want to go where they might not get what they're looking for because then they have to go somewhere else, and the one thing that they can't afford to waste anymore is time.

And then you have your upper end, stores like Nordstroms, Lord & Taylor, Bloomingdales, Neiman Marcus, Banana Republic, Abercrombie & Fitch, American Eagle Outfitters. Do you remember those midrange, mid-priced department stores? They're like dinosaurs. Those are the places you used to go when you were a kid. Your parents used to drag you there to get your clothes. Remember those places?

Every single major city in America had two, three, or four of those midrange department stores. When I worked in the dress business in the Garment Center back in the 70s to the early 80s, that's all we sold to, those midrange department stores all across the country.

In every single one of those cities, that four or three became maybe one or two because they either went out of business or they merged. Why? It's because they were just pretty good. Because their prices were higher than the discounters, but their service was not as good. Their prices were lower than the best guys, but their service wasn't nearly as good. Their selection wasn't as good. They didn't have all that stuff.

Now you've got to decide. You can be the cheapest or the best. Where do you want to be? I'll tell you where I wouldn't want to be. I would never want to be the cheapest. To me, there is absolutely, positively no percentage in being the cheapest. I would only want to be the best, and I'm going to tell you why. In fact, I'm going to give you three reasons today why you never want to be the price company. You never want to be the price person.

The first reason you don't want to be the price company, the first reason you never want to be the price person is very simple, because price is without a doubt the single easiest thing for competition to duplicate. Any idiot can drop their price. You don't have to be a genius to do that.

But what is tough for the competition to duplicate? Extraordinary quality, service, convenience and value. Why? Because extraordinary quality, service, convenience, and value require the most effort. Most people and most companies are not willing to put forth the extra effort. Why? It's because it is *hard*.

I'm going to tell you what I tell my kids all the time. They come to me, and say, "But, Dad, I can't do this. It's too hard." I don't know why they keep coming to me and saying that because they know exactly what I'm going to say every single time, which is, "Yes, I know it's hard, and you know why it's hard? Because if this stuff were easy, everyone would do it."

You see, it's the hard that makes you great. It's the willingness to do the hard that makes you great, and it's the willingness to do the hard that will always separate you from the competition because most people are only willing to do the easy, and that means dropping price.

We are talking about how we create value rather than sell price. We are talking about how we differentiate ourselves from the competition, and we're talking about the three reasons why you don't want a sell price or be known as the price person or the price company, why you want to be the best. As you see, the first reason is that price is the single easiest thing for your competition to duplicate.

The second reason that you don't want to be the price company or the price person is because price is not the single biggest reason why people buy. Most people are not as worried about the price, but they do want extraordinary quality, service, convenience, and value. They want you to be able to save them time and make their lives easier, and more than ever they want, demand, and need your knowledge, expertise, information, and education. They're not as worried about price, yet many customers end up buying price.

Why is this? You know why customers buy price? They buy price because they find it so difficult to find all that other stuff. The biggest reason a customer will buy price is because far too often it is the only alternative that we leave them with.

Think about all the times that you have bought price. I am not saying that people want to overpay. Nobody wants to overpay, but there's a big difference between value and price. I don't mind paying more if I know that I'm always getting more, but I'm not going to pay more and get less. Nobody wants to do that.

I'm going to look for price if all else fails, and that's what everybody else does, but price is not the uppermost thing in people's mind. In fact, why do the sales of luxury cars always outpace the sales of all the other cars? SUVs are not the cheapest cars. If price is what drove car sales, then why didn't everybody buy a Yugo?

People want quality, and they'll pay for quality. They'll pay for service, convenience. They'll pay for all that stuff. They'll pay for value. If they perceive they're getting value, if they know they're getting value, they'll pay more for it.

Let's pick on an easy target. Let's pick on the airlines. I don't think anybody can beat the airlines when it comes to stupidity in sales and marketing. I remember reading an article a while ago, where American Airlines was again crying and moaning about business being down. The new chairman and the new CEO of American Airlines, was complaining that people were flying on discount airlines simply because of the cheap prices.

As a former flyer on American Airlines, I can tell you that is *not* the biggest reason. I used to fly American Airlines all the time, over 100,000 miles a year. I've done over 4 million miles in my career on American Airlines. I was executive platinum on American Airlines. You know what executive platinum means? That means I was two notches above dirt. That means they actually had to talk to me sometimes when I called, sometimes had to be nice to me.

I was not flying on regular tickets or cheap tickets. I was flying on first-class tickets. You know what happened about two years ago? I stopped flying American Airlines, and I started flying Southwest Airlines. Why? Because I got sick and tired of having to worry that I was going to get there on time. I got sick and tired of having to worry that I was going to make my connection. I got sick and tired of dealing with people who couldn't care less, who were more concerned about their comfort than my comfort.

I had an instance where I flew into O'Hare Airport in Chicago. My flight arrived on time, in fact a few minutes early, and I still missed my connection. You know why? I'll tell you why. Because when we got into Chicago, they couldn't get the jetway to work. They made us sit on that plane for 45 minutes while they tried to get the jetway to work.

I suggested to the flight attendant, I said, "Listen, instead of making us sit here and miss our connections, why don't you guys just roll a step truck up to the plane, get us off, and once we're off then figure out how to work the jetway?" All she could say to me, the flight attendant, was, "Well, you know, we all have some place to go." I'm saying, well, hold it a second. You might have some place to go and I might have some place to go, but if you don't get where you're going, you still get paid. If I don't get where I'm going, I don't get paid, and I'm not going to lose money because you guys don't care.

I got into another fight with them, and finally I just decided that's it, I'm out of here. Now, I fly Southwest. While my contract on my speaking engagement still says I can fly first class, I still choose to fly Southwest most of the time. For over two years of flying Southwest Airlines—and I'm knocking on wood here, folks, but I have never been late. I have never missed a connection.

I even do something I would never do on any other airline, I check my bag. Why? Because I trust them.

Why? When I fly Southwest Airlines, it's the only time I ever get the feeling that I'm flying an airline that wants to be on time as much as I do. Those people that work for Southwest want to be on time as much as I do.

We go away for Christmas every year, my wife and I and my kids. We go to California to visit my sister-in-law. We were flying back from California at Christmas time and the heightened terror alerts and really tough security at LAX, and it's a mess. It's December 29th. We get to the airport, and there's a line. There must have been at least 100 people in front of us on line to check in at the Southwest counter.

We got to the front of that line, we got to the ticket counter within eight, nine minutes. I used my stopwatch. I time this stuff, and I'll tell you why, because you look behind that counter, they had 15, 16 people working behind that counter checking people in. Now, you go to any other airline, and you tell me how many people are sitting behind that counter. Usually three, and usually only two of them are working because one of them is a supervisor standing there with a cup of coffee saying, "Boy, that's a long line."

So, it's not just the price. It's not the price, and I'll tell you why. I know it's not the price with Southwest Airlines because I don't pay for the tickets. My clients do, and yet I choose to fly them. It's not the price, why most people buy. It's only the price when all else fails.

I did a speech for a group of people called the National Sporting Goods Association. My audience was small, only about 50 to 100 people, but it was all CEOs and the next level under, CEOs and presidents of top sporting goods chains in America.

This was very interesting. In my research on their organization, they sent me this book which was actually a ten-year research project that they had done on the sporting goods retail industry. It was ten things that they had found, ten trends they found in the industry over the decade of the 90s.

One of the trends that they found in the industry was very interesting. It was that every single sporting goods chain whose main marketing thrust was to sell price— their biggest benefit was that they were the cheapest— every company that did that in the 90s went out of business. That's right, because while price is important, it's not as important as value.

Price is good for one thing; it's good for getting people in the door. It's good for getting them to try what you have. But while price might get them in, price is not what keeps them coming back. It's value that does that. It is quality, service, convenience, and value. It's saving me time, making my life easier. It's all that other stuff. So, it's not just the price, folks. It's not just the price.

The third reason why you never want to be the price person, why you never want to be the price company, again, very simple, it's because price never makes you indispensable to your clients. Price only makes you highly replaceable. If the biggest benefit of buying from you is that you have the best price, if that is the only benefit of buying from you then what happens when someone comes along and is cheaper? Because you know that's always going to be the case. Some people might drop their price and take a loss just to take your business from you.

If the only benefit you're giving to your customers is the price, if that's the only reason they buy from you, then that's just making you replaceable. When you are doing all the other stuff, when you are giving them the quality, service, convenience and value, when you are saving them time and making their lives easier, when you are their knowledge person, when you are their expert advisor and resource, then that is hard to replace you. How many people like that do you think they can go out and find?

That's pretty hard to do, so it's going to make you indispensable to your customers. Look around you. Look at companies that understand this. Look at companies that understand that whole process of knowing who the customer is and what they really, truly want.

Southwest Airlines is one of them. They know that the biggest thing you want when you fly is obviously safety, but also, you want to get there. You want to get there on time. You don't want to have to hassle. You don't want to have to worry. You want it to be as easy as possible.

I've seen them turn a plane around in seven minutes. From the time that plane came in, from the time the first person got off until the time the first person got on, I've seen them do that in seven minutes. They get you in, they get you out, they get you on your way, and that's what I want because, to me, in my business, it doesn't matter how good my speech is if I don't get there. That's what I'm looking for.

Look at other companies that do it right. Look at other companies who know what they're doing. Another interesting company to me is a company that built their success on doing it right and then hit a real rough patch because they forgot about all that stuff they did that got them there. You know what that company is? It's McDonald's.

McDonald's is a fascinating company to me. Talk about being the best. Let's face it, McDonald's is number one. Number one in their industry. As you all know, that is a very competitive industry. I don't think there is any more competitive an industry than fast food.

They're number one in their industry. They're number one forever. I can't remember when they weren't number one in that industry. They're number one for not just a million years, but they're number one by a million miles. They're the biggest company in the fast food industry.

How did they do it? They did it by understanding who their customer is and what they really, truly want. If you watched McDonald's in the past, what got them there was all that other stuff. If you watched McDonald's commercials in the past, McDonald's hardly ever advertised price, something they started doing the last few years, and that has not helped them at all.

When they started out, they never used to advertise price. They used to do things like food, folks, and fun, Mac Tonight. My favorite, "Have you had your break today?" Now, think about that. How clever is that, "Have you had your break today?"

Think about your life. Think about the lives of all the people you know. Think about the lives of your customers. What do you think all these people would rather have, a cheap hamburger or a break? I think they'd rather have a break, and McDonald's understands that. They understand who the customer is and what they really, truly want.

You know what their corporate motto is? Q, S, C, and V: quality, service, convenience and value. Notice it doesn't say quality, service, convenience, and cheap. It doesn't even say quality, service, convenience, and food. They say quality, service, convenience, and value.

They understand. They always did. They got away from that. McDonald's never used to sell food. They started selling food, they started selling price, and that has hurt them over the past few years. Now they're trying to get away from that again, trying to get back to what they've always done best, which is sell McDonald's, which is sell the experience.

Let's think about it. All of you with kids, have you ever taken your kids out to eat there? Come on, we've all done it. Now, when you make the decision to go, who really makes the decision? The kids do. It has nothing to do with you.

Another thing McDonald's understands is that they have different sets of customers, just like you do, and those different sets of customers buy for totally different reasons, just like your customers do. They have adults, they have kids, and both sets of customers buy for totally different reasons.

Has this ever happened to you? Has one of your kids ever come up to you and said, "Mom, Dad, today, let's go to Burger King. I just found out, we can save a quarter"? Of course not. Believe me, that's never going to happen, never will.

But you ever notice something? Whenever the kids eat this stuff, they always get the same thing, hamburger, French fries, and Coke; hamburger, French fries, and Coke. I don't care what anybody says, but to me a hamburger, French fries, and Coke is a hamburger, French fries, and Coke and I don't care where the heck you take the kids.

Now that was a problem for McDonald's. They didn't want people saying that. They didn't want people believing that because they know if people believe a hamburger, French fries, and Coke is a hamburger, French fries, and Coke, that's like saying life insurance is life insurance; an airline is an airline; a computer company is a computer company. It's all the same. If people really believe it's all the same, then what do they buy? That's right, they buy price.

Like you, McDonald's did not want to be the cheapest. They wanted to be the best. They also knew something else. They also knew that if all the kids wanted was a hamburger, French fries, and Coke, then that takes the decision out of the kids' hands, because when your kids come to you and say, "Mom, Dad, I want a hamburger, French fries, and Coke, well, now the decision is yours. You can go anywhere, and you might go to the cheapest.

What does McDonald's decide? We will no longer sell the children a hamburger, French fries, and Coke, and they don't. Now, they sell them a Happy Meal.

You know what a Happy Meal is? It's a hamburger, French fries, and a Coke. Except they take this $0.05 toy, they shove it in a $0.04 box with little puzzles on the box, and the kids love it. Why? Because McDonald's knew. They understood. They knew who the customer was and what they really, truly wanted, and they knew, they knew the kids didn't want the food. The kids wanted the toy. The kids wanted the box. You know why? Because kids don't buy food. Kids buy fun.

They figure they can get food anywhere. Some of them can even get it at home. Now, the kids no longer go up to their parents and say, "Mom, Dad, I want a hamburger, French fries, and Coke, and leave the decision to you, and we can go anywhere. They now say, "Mom, Dad, I want a Happy Meal." Now you've got one choice, McDonald's, and they get all the business. Why? Because they understood who the customer was and what they really, truly wanted.

My next question to you is this: What is your Happy Meal? What is it that you are willing to do for all your customers, for all your clients, for all your prospects, that no one else is willing to do? How are you differentiating yourself from the competition?

What a lot of salespeople don't understand, what a lot of companies don't even understand is what's going on in the marketplace as far as demographics. I want you to understand what the demographic changes are in American society in the past 20, 30 years. It has changed who your customers are. It has changed what customers buy. And most importantly, it has changed I customers buy.

Think about it. What has been the single biggest demographic change in this country in the last 20, 30 years? It's been women in the workplace. The fact of women in the workplace is the single biggest demographic change in this country in the last 20, 30 years, and it has changed all the rules of the game.

That's right. As far as salespeople go, as far as selling goes, it's changed all the rules of the game, because it's changed who your customers are. It's changed what they buy, how they buy, but most importantly it's changed why they buy. And not just why women buy; it has changed why men buy too.

It has changed people's priorities. Think about this. Go back 30 years. You know, 30 years ago, most women were not working. Most women were home raising families, and what did families have a lot more of back then that they don't have any of now? Time. That's right, time.

Think about this, why do you think stores are open on Sundays? Why are supermarkets open 24 hours a day? Is it because people enjoy buying milk at two in the morning? No, it's because they don't have time. Hey, years ago, people used to get their errands done on Wednesday afternoon, Thursday mornings. They didn't have to worry about stores being open late. They had time. That's right.

You know what women used to do a lot more of back then that they don't do hardly any of now or not nearly as much of now, and not in the same way? Shop. That's right, shop. Think about this, women shop a lot more like men now. Women don't shop like they used to.

Women used to go from store to store to store to store to store to store, bought anything they wanted. Sometimes they'd buy things they didn't want. You know why? They had time to go back the next day. They'd return it. But they don't do that anymore, and you know why? They're busy. They're very busy.

Why are they busy? Because they've got jobs, and they don't just have jobs, they have careers. They own businesses. Women now own 38% of all the businesses in America. That's right.

Women employ 25% of all the workers in America, and those businesses generate $3 trillion in sales. That has changed who the customer is. It was so easy if you were a salesperson 25, 30 years ago. You'd walk into the office, and ask the first woman you saw to get the boss. Try that now and see what happens. You'll be in and out of there fast. You might go out head first, but you'll be out fast.

Right now there are more women in med school than men. There are more women in law school right now than men. In fact, on the undergraduate college level, the ratio of women to men is somewhere around 3:2. So, for those of you guys that couldn't get a date in college, go back.

What has this created? This has created a huge society of two-paycheck households. That's right, two-paycheck households. In fact, in an article in *Fortune* magazine a couple of years ago, they noted that 84% of all two-parent households in this country were also two-paycheck households. What does that tell us?

That tells us that these people have money coming in. They've got money coming in from two different places. So, money is not the major issue, but what is the major issue if everybody's working? Obviously, the major issue is time. And folks, these are your customers. These are your clients. These are your prospects. Think about it.

Think about what they're looking for. What don't they have is time. People are stressed out at work. People are stressed out at home. The last person they're going to allow to stress them out is someone who's trying to sell them something, and that's you. Think about it.

Let's look at these people. Let's look at their lives. Let's look at the average day of the average two-income, two-paycheck household. Forget, by the way, another big demographic change. Forget about the single-parent households because they have no time whatsoever.

But let's look at these two-income, two-paycheck households. They get up in the morning, have to get dressed, and have to go to work. But wait, they've got to wake the kids, have to get them dressed. They have to feed them breakfast and get them off to school. Kids don't come home from school at 2:00 or 3:00 in the after-noon anymore. Why? There's nobody home.

So, where do they go? They go to daycare. They go to babysitting. They go to an after-school program or maybe they go to one of the many thousands of activi-ties that we sign them up for. Nine-year-olds out there are carrying around Palm Pilots. Certainly the world has changed. Back when I was in elementary school, I used to go home for lunch.

Every kid in my class went home for lunch. Everyone's mother was home. Some kids even got a hot lunch—not me, but some did. But that doesn't happen anymore. By the time these kids get picked up, it could be 5:30, 6:00 at night. You want to know the interesting statistic? 1996 was the first year ever in the history of this country that restaurants did more business than supermarkets and food stores combined. What does that tell you? That tells you what people are looking for. Are they looking to save money, or are they looking to save time? They are looking for convenience.

So, the kids get picked up, it's 5:30, 6:00 at night. Now, you have to feed them and get them home. Then they have to do their homework. Then you have to get them off to bed. By the time some of these parents have a chance to relax, it's 9:30, 10:00 at night. Are they going to feel like dealing with a salesperson now?

These are your customers. These are your clients. These are your prospects. What are you doing to save them time? What are you doing to make their lives easier? What are you doing to take the fear, the stress, and the anxiety out of the sales situation? Because their lives are stressed. Whether at work or at home, they're under stress.

If they work for a large corporation, they've probably gone through a couple rounds of downsizing, so where they had seven, eight people in their department, maybe they have three or four people in their department. People are working harder. They're doing more than one job now at work.

They're stressed out at work. They're stressed out at home. The last person they're going to want to stress them out is you, someone who's trying to sell them something. I'll tell you right now, if you can give your clients just two things, just two things, you will be successful. You know what those two things are? Speed and ease.

If you just sell speed and ease, you will be successful. Get it for me, get it for me fast, and get it for me with the least amount of hassle as possible, because that is what I want. That is what I need. I don't want to be hassled. I have enough hassles in my life. I don't need hassles from people who are taking my money. Sell me speed and ease.

Let's talk about gasoline, a commodity we might think would be sold more on price than anything else. But how do they market, these retail gas stations? What's the biggest thing they use to market their gas? It's pump, pay, and go, right? Pump, pay, and go.

You don't have to stop. You don't have to go inside. It's just pump, pay, and go. Stick in your credit card, pull it out, pump in the gas, and get the heck out of there. That's right, speed and ease. It's so easy.

Shell had a great ad campaign not too long ago. It was called "Moving at the speed of life." They showed this woman dressed in her business suit, driving an SUV, working mother, obviously, coming up to that pump, just *boom, boom, boom*—pump, pay and go, because she is busy at work. She is busy at home. The last thing she needs to do is stop, walk inside, deal with who's working inside, then have to go out and have to pump the gas, then have to go back inside, get a receipt.

It is one big hassle. Speed and ease, this is what clients are looking for, folks. This is what clients want. How can you save me time? Can you make my life easier? Can you take the fear of stress and anxiety out of the buying process? Because I don't have time.

I don't like to make a lot of guarantees, but here is an exception. One thing I can guarantee you not a single one of your customers wants, and it is this: They do not want to be an expert on what it is that you do. That's what they have you for, to be their expert, their advisor, and their resource.

Why? They don't have the time or the inclination to be an expert on what it is that you do. If you want to sell me something, my policy is that I do nothing. If I have to do any part of your job to help you sell me, then I want to split the commission because I already have a job. I don't need another job that I don't get paid for because I don't have the time or the inclination to be an expert on what you do. That's what I have you for, for your knowledge, expertise, information, education.

If you cannot do that for me, then I don't need you. I can get all that from the internet. The internet is a wonderful invention. The internet is one of the greatest inventions of the 20th century. I am amazed every day. But what is one of the biggest problems with the internet? It's that all the internet really does is to just throw information at you.

But here's a bigger problem. What do most salespeople do? That's right; they just throw information at you. My challenge to you, if you want to be successful, if you want to be great in this new century, then you have to be better than my computer. If you cannot be better than my computer, then I don't need you.

You see, you've got to be able to make that information easy for me. You've got to able to organize that information and act on that information and deliver it to me in a way that I cannot only understand it quickly and easily, but that I can implement it quickly and easily, because if you can do that, then you become valuable to me. If you become valuable to me, then your price is immaterial because I cannot find enough people of value who I can deal with.

Let me tell you what's going on out there with the internet. The internet is doing to salespeople what automation did to the factory floor 20 years ago. It is getting rid of the unskilled. Think about that. The internet is doing a real favor for companies because it's getting rid of the poor-to-mediocre salesperson.

I don't need the poor-to-mediocre salesperson. I don't need someone who just hands me a brochure and expects me to figure out what it's all about. I can get that on the internet, and I don't have to pay commissions. I don't have to pay for those salaries. I can get better prices because of the lower overhead.

Do you remember what happened on the factory floor back in the early 80s, how the sky was falling? People were telling us, "All the manufacturing jobs are going overseas." They're still saying that, "We're no longer going to manufacture in this country anymore."

Do you remember when the prediction was that the Japanese were going to eat our lunch? We're going to become a nation of hamburger flippers—remember that? Well, here we are decades later, and guess what, we manufacture more in this country than we ever have. We have buried the Japanese economy. We're not only number one, our economy's not only number one in the world, but we're number one by a million miles. The Japanese economy hasn't come out of their funk in over ten years. It's only starting now.

We are still manufacturing, but we're manufacturing with fewer people because we're more productive because as we keep evolving as a society. If you expect our standard of living to rise, you've got to keep changing with it. The people on the factory floor are more knowledgeable than ever. The people on the factory floor are more educated than ever. They're more highly skilled than ever, and because of that, they're more highly paid than ever.

It's the same thing with the great salesperson. If you are willing to be a great salesperson, if you are willing to do all those things, you become more valuable.

A few years ago I flew to Monte Carlo to speak to the 50 top producers in a company of a couple thousand salespeople. They said to me, "Many of our consultants are telling us that in the 21st century there will be no more need for face-to-face salespeople." I said, "Well, I don't know about that." I'll tell you what there won't be a need for, there won't be a need for poor-to-mediocre face-to-face salespeople, but people still want to deal with a person. Every single survey I've seen on customer habits tells me they want to deal with a person, but they want to deal with great people.

If you are willing to be that great person, if you are willing to be an expert advisor and a resource, if you are willing to be someone who saves people time and makes their lives easier, if you are willing to be someone who sells knowledge, expertise, information, education, you have an opportunity to be more successful than you've ever been. You know why? Because as we have seen, the supply of people like you is low, but the demand for people like you is still high. When demand for something is high and supply of it is low, you can write your own price.

See, quality, service, convenience and value—save me time, make my life easier. Be my expert advisor and resource. Sell me knowledge, expertise, information, and education. These are the things that the customer of the 21st century is demanding, and these are things that the companies and the salespeople of the 21st century must be able to deliver.

The Three S's of Success

See it, start it, and sustain it! If you've come this far, I'm going to assume you not only like the book but have gotten something out of it. This last chapter ties everything up in one nice neat package, because if we analyze the three S's, see it, start it, and sustain it, we see they really are a microcosm of everything you need to do to be successful. So, listen, learn, and most of all, do something about it.

Before we begin with the three S's of success I want to talk about personal responsibility. I'm a big believer in the fact that each and every one of us has control over our lives and our destiny. I believe that we control the things that happen to us in our lives, our careers and our destinies and that no one else is in control. We truly have to believe that.

I am really distressed about what I see all around me, what I call the growing of the victim mentality. We see it more and more every day, people who blame outside forces for their plight while rejecting the proposition that nothing succeeds like hard work. Victims take comfort in placing the burden of failure or lack of effort on others rather than looking to themselves, digging in, working hard, and fighting back.

People blame their teachers. My teacher hates me; my boss hates me. That's the reason I'm not getting ahead. The customers don't like me. I don't get the good leads; I get all the companies that can't pass the credit check. Nobody likes me around here. They are constantly blaming and making excuses.

We see people that have smoked for years that are now suing cigarette companies, even though cigarette packs for over 30 years have warned us about the dangers of smoking. Politicians are telling us the reason that kids and adults are obese is because of the labels on the food, as if they're eating the labels and not just the food. It's unbelievable to me, people suing McDonald's because they claim they didn't know that eating cheeseburgers, Big Macs, and French fries every day was going to make them fat.

But the best, example of this attitude has to be the following story about a man from Fond du Lac, Wisconsin who is accusing his cable company of addicting him, his wife, and his kids to TV and threatening to sue. He said his family's viewing habits forced on him by cable TV, caused his wife to become overweight and his children to grow lazy. But wait, it gets better. He said his cable company is liable because the company continued to provide him service when he requested its cancellation. How long

did the company continue to provide him service after he requested cancellation? How about four years?

I want to know why didn't he just disconnect the box or cut the cord. When asked that, his response was that he thought that such an act was illegal. He thought someone's going to kick down his door and say, you canceled your service, and you shouldn't disconnect this by yourself. He did not wish to face prosecution. Even if he is right, I ask why not just simply refuse to watch? He said his remote control exerted a power so irresistible, he could not force himself to stop watching.

There's more. He claims that he previously give up drinking and smoking, habits he resumed after the installation and the pernicious influence of cable TV.

Now he's retreating. His wife became angry when he called her fat. He claimed he really didn't say that his kids were lazy, although that's what the police report says.

The good news is the cable company finally discontinued his service. But even after they discontinued his service, he bought a special antenna so he could watch the Green Bay Packers. Now, I'm wondering, if the Packers blow their games will he sue them Packers for emotional distress?

See It

The choices are always up to you. This is so important to keep in mind as we talk about the three S's of success. You must be able to see it. See yourself successful, because if you can see yourself successful, you can *be* suc-

cessful. You have to be able to create vision. Successful people create visions.

First and foremost, they create visions for themselves. They create visions for their lives. They create visions for their careers, and because they're able to create visions for themselves, they're also able to create and communicate visions to others. That's what makes them leaders.

If you can see yourself doing something in your mind, then you can do it. If you cannot see yourself doing something in your mind, how can you possibly be able to do it in real life? Let me pose this question to you: Have you ever used this expression or heard someone say, "I can't imagine doing that in my wildest dreams"? Well, if you can't do it in your wildest dreams, what makes you think you can do it in real life?

You know as well as I do it's a lot easier to do this stuff in our dreams. So, just see it. See yourself successful. Visualize it. What are you trying to do? You're trying to create a picture in your mind of what you want your success to be.

I'm going to pose another question to you. We just took a look at the victim mentality. I want you to think about this person we all know. I call them excuse-makers.

You know the people I'm talking about. Like I was just talking, the ones who always tell us how successful they could have been, but they have no luck. They never catch a break.

We all know people like that. Nobody likes them, right? Everybody's always plotting against them, they never get the good leads, they whine. You're lucky, I'm

not a lucky person, and circumstances are beyond my control. Everything is beyond their control. We all know people like that. We've all worked with people like that.

In New York City we have a saying that goes like this, "Everyone in New York knows somebody else who could have bought a building 30 years ago for $9." We all know somebody like that.

They always say the same thing, "See that building over there? Thirty years ago, I could have bought that building—$9." "Well why didn't you?" "Lousy jerks, they talked me out of it." "Well, why don't you buy it now?" "No, it's too late now." You know what? That guy's right. It's too late. You know why? He believes it's too late.

Let's say the excuse-makers are right. Let's say that everybody's plotting against them. Let's say they have no luck. Even though we know they're wrong, let's say they're right. I still have one question for all the excuse-makers: How come you still cannot even see yourself successful? I mean, nobody stops you from dreaming, folks, and I'll tell you this, if you don't have good dreams, all that's left are nightmares.

See it. See yourself successful. Visualize it. Create that picture of what you want your success to be in your mind.

I've worked with so many people like that. My first sales job ever was back in July of 1973, which seems like a million years ago. At that time, I took a job as a salesman for a dress manufacturer in New York City's Garment Center.

I don't know if you know anything about the dress manufacturing business, but I can tell you that in this

business, they have a saying, "You can't do business in December." Everybody knows those sayings. Every company has one of those sayings. Every industry has one. I call them the "you can't do business in" sayings.

You can't do business in December. Nobody wants to talk to you because they're getting ready for the holidays. You can't do business in January. Nobody wants to talk to you in January. Why? Because nobody has any money left over from the holidays. You can't do business in the summer. Nobody talks to you in the summer because everybody's getting ready to go on vacation.

You're not going to do business on a Friday. Nobody's going to talk to you on a Friday. They're not going to pick up the phone on a Friday because they're getting ready to go away for the weekend. You certainly can't do business on a Monday. Who's going to talk to you on a Monday? They just got back from the weekend. They don't pick up the phone. In fact, I'm convinced there's this one Wednesday in May that's the only good time of the year to do business.

So you see, if you let them, other people will stop you every way they can. You know why? Because they don't see themselves successful. They only see themselves failing. You know what they always need? They always need a reason.

You know, we've just come through an economic slump in the last couple of years which, obviously, I really believe is over. I see the economy picking up. I see lots of evidence of the economy really getting strong. One of the things I've noticed in my travels and working with

companies and speaking to large organizations are the attitudes during down economic times.

I can tell you that the biggest reason that people do not do business during down economic periods is that they give up because it's easy to give up. They have a built-in excuse. They have the economy. They can always go back to their boss and say, "Well, you know, I tried, but nobody's buying out there because, you see, the economy is bad."

I am convinced that during down economic times, salespeople stop selling long before customers stop buying. You see, I am also convinced that the best time to be out there, the best time to really push harder than ever is during a down economic time. Why? Because all your competition has given up. If you're out there, you're the only one out there, and all the business is yours.

You might not get as much business as before because of the economic period. I think down economic periods are the best time to increase market share because everybody else is sitting in the coffee shop writing their excuses down on a nice, big, long legal pad. So, see it. You have to see yourself successful. You have to visualize it. You have to take that picture in your mind of what you want your success to be.

And once you've done that, once you've seen it, once you've visualized it, once you've taken that picture of success in your mind—you know, a lot of you have done it. If you've listened to me talk about goal setting, this is where goal setting starts, when you take that vision. This is where the goal starts. You take that vision in your mind; you create the picture of it. I you can see yourself doing something in your mind, you can do it. How can you really do it if you can't even see yourself doing it?

That's where the goal comes from. When I talked about goals, I talked about being specific. That's how you become specific about your goals, by first creating the vision in your mind. If you can see the goal in your mind, if you can create a picture of the goal in your mind, then it becomes that much easier to create a specific goal on paper. So, you take that vision, you take that vision that you see in your mind, you take that picture, and then you write it down.

Now you've got the goal. Then you take the goal, and you plan it out. We've talked about that. You have your vision. You have your goal. You take your plan, and you have to see yourself successful. Most people don't see themselves successful. Most people see themselves failing, and that's why they don't achieve what they want out of life. They're always worried about *I can't do that*. That's the first attitude, I can't do that, rather than I can.

Start It

Now you've got the goal, you've got the plan, you've got the vision. Now we're ready for the second "S" which very simply says you have to start. You have to be able to act. You have to be able to do something.

The problem is most people don't act. You've got the goal, you've got the plan, but they never take that first step. The key is to start to act, to do something. I will tell you right now that you have 24 hours to act on a good idea. If you do absolutely nothing about a good idea within 24 hours, that good idea is dead. Now I'm not saying that you have to take a good idea and do everything about it within 24 hours—no, but I'm telling you that you must take at least one small action step, anything, any kind of action step.

Let's say your idea is I want to start a regular program of exercise right away. I haven't exercised in years. I want to start. Even if you just went out today and walked around the block, you took that first step. I don't care how big or how small that first step is, I just care that you take it and you do it within 24 hours just to keep the excitement going. Because when are we most excited about our good ideas? You know as well as I do it's when we first get them. That's when we're most excited about our good ideas.

If we let them lie around for a couple of weeks, then we just spend time convincing ourselves why it won't work. So take that first step, act, do something.

I have this philosophy, and I really believe this. I truly believe that there is no such thing as a bad idea. To me, the only bad ideas are the ones that (a) are not acted upon, or (b) are not acted upon properly.

Think about it. Think about all the stupid stuff you've seen in the world that has been incredibly successful. Take for instance, the pet rock. Does it get much dumber than the pet rock? How about Teenage Mutant Ninja Turtles? How's that for a dumb idea? Someone would have come to you and said I've got a good idea that's going to make us all money, Teenage Mutant Ninja

Turtles. Think about it—one of the longest-running fads in the history of this country. They made billions on this thing. It was four green turtles that live in a sewer. They were named after Renaissance artists—Michelangelo, Raphael, Leonardo and Donatello.

They only eat pizza, and they were superheroes, a really crazy idea. When my son was a kid, we spent a fortune on Teenage Mutant Ninja Turtle items—toys, games, videos, clothing, movies. You name it, they had it.

We're talking about no such thing as a bad idea. How about *SpongeBob SquarePants*?

SpongeBob SquarePants is a cartoon, about a sponge named Bob. He's not really square. He's more rectangular, but I think SpongeBob SquarePants sounds better than Sponge Bob Rectangular Pants, so that's why they call him SpongeBob SquarePants.

He lives under the sea. He's a sponge. Not a sponge like you'd see swimming in the ocean. He's the sort of sponge that you'd see on your kitchen sink, the kind that you clean up spills and garbage with. He's this square sponge with these square pants and little eyes. He lives under the water, and he's got these goofy friends. It's so stupid, it's unbelievable. It's one of the dumbest ideas that you've ever seen in your entire life.

I can't believe the money they're making—the toys, the games, the clothing, the towels, the videos, the movies. It's a cartoon show. It seems to be on about 20 times a day, and it's about a sponge.

Let's take a hypothetical instance. Let's say a friend of yours approaches and says, listen, I've got the greatest idea in the world. Now, I know I've come to you with some crazy ideas before, but I've got an idea here that is going to make us rich beyond our wildest dreams. I'm going to give you an opportunity to be my partner on this.

Wait until you hear this. This is so good; you will beg me to write a check. All I need from you is $10,000. We've got to get this started. If you give me $10,000, you're in. You become my partner. It's the greatest idea in the world. It's called *SpongeBob SquarePants*. What do you think of that? Okay, I know what you're saying, but let me tell you what it is. Let me tell you what it is. Okay, here it is.

This guy, his name is Bob, and he's a sponge. He's a sponge. He's a square sponge, the kind of sponge you see on your kitchen sink when you mop up spills, but this is better because this sponge, he's like a guy. He's got eyes, and he's got a mouth. He wears square pants. He lives under the water, and he's got these really goofy friends.

We're going to make cartoons. We're going to make games. We're going to make videos, and all I need is $10,000 from you. You buy in, you can be my partner. *SpongeBob SquarePants*, what do you think? So, are you in?

Question: What would you have said? You probably would've said, "What are you, nuts? Get out of here." I'm sure probably plenty of other people said that too. In fact, the people that developed Teenage Mutant Ninja Turtles were thrown out of almost every toy company in the world. Teenage Mutant Ninja Turtles was developed by a couple of nerdy guys in a garage who first started out with an underground comic book about Teenage Mutant

Ninja Turtles. They approached all these people, who threw them out. They end up making billions.

In fact, here's a quote from Hasbro who said to those guys, "No one will ever buy little green turtles that live in a sewer." How'd you like to be the executive that made that decision? See, folks, there's no such thing as a bad idea, but you've got to start. You've got to act. You've got to do something.

Sustain It

You have seen it. You've seen yourself successful. You visualized it. You created that picture of what you want your success to be in your mind. You've even taken that vision. You've described it. You've focused on it. You've written it down. You've created a goal, and you made a plan. Then you took that first step. You started. You acted. You did something.

Now we come to the third "S" in the word success. This is where the truly successful will break away from the pack. This is where the 3% will always be great, will leave the other 97% behind, because you see, the third "S" in the word success very simply says you've got to be able to sustain the effort.

It's called persistence. Because I'll tell you right now, people never, ever fail. They don't fail. They just stop trying. Folks, as long as you keep going out there day after day after day after day, you are constantly giving yourself the opportunity to be successful, to be great, and to be the best, but you see, the second you stop, you have taken away any opportunity you ever had to be successful or to be great.

Yes, I know what's going to happen, and you know what's going to happen. We all know what's going to happen. There's going to be road blocks. Come on, there's always going to be roadblocks. Everybody knows that. I'm sure pretty much everybody reading this has probably experienced some of those roadblocks at one time or another in their life, career, or business.

The interesting thing about roadblocks is this, it's that the choice is always up to you. I mean, you can sit around, and you can wait for someone else to clear that roadblock for you, or you can go over it, around it, or through it, because no matter what you do, there will always be roadblocks.

Let's recall the story about Peter Rosengard who got into the *Guinness Book of World Records* for selling the largest life insurance policy on record at that time. He sold a $100 million life insurance policy on the life of entertainment entrepreneur, David Geffen.

It wasn't so much the fact of the sale that impresses me. What really impressed me was how he did it, because how he did it is the perfect example of the three "S"s. It's the perfect example of someone who only saw himself successful, perfect example of someone who really created a picture in his mind of what he wanted success to be. He focused. He described. Then he acted. He took that first step, and he never stopped. He just kept going and going and going until he was successful.

This sale illustrates all three S's of success in one microcosm. It was also the perfect example of someone who never doubted himself. He never jumped to conclusions. He never assumed. He did not prejudge himself or his customer. Basically this is the story of someone who only saw a prospect with a need. He only saw someone who needed what he had. His attitude was, they need what I have. They will buy it from someone. They might as well buy it from me.

Now, one of the best things about this whole story was that Peter actually sold this policy off of a cold call. That's amazing to me—$100 million policy off of a cold call.

Not once, through the entire process, did Peter ever stop seeing himself successful. So, see it. See yourself successful. Visualize it. Create that picture of what you want your success to be in your mind. Then once you've seen it, visualized it, created that picture, you write it down. You set your goal, you plan it out, and then you start, just like Peter did. You act, you do something. Then once you've started, acted, do something, you've got to keep going, because I'll tell you what, you've got to persist, sustain the effort.

The beauty of life is that life is not a sprint. Life is a marathon, and that is really the beauty of life. You know why? Because in order to be successful in a sprint, you've got to flat-out win it, but in order to be successful in a marathon, all you've got to do is finish.

Think about it, do any of you out there run marathons? If you know anybody that runs marathons, do you ever ask them if they've won? Come on, no one ever wins those. It's always some super runner from Africa who wins. Yet, aren't we always impressed when they tell you that they finished? Of course we're impressed! Why? It's because anyone can finish a sprint. Most anyone can last 100 yards, but not everyone has what it takes to hang in there for 26 miles. All you have to do is finish in order to be successful since most of your competition is going to give up before that race ever ends. Most of the competition does not have what it takes to hang in there for 26 miles because they do not have the commitment to go out there day after day after day after day. They just don't understand that success is not just a one-time thing.

Those of you that have ever been successful know that it is a lot easier to get to be successful than it is to stay successful. It is a lot easier to get to the top than it is to stay on top. Most people are going to relax after their first taste of success because they don't understand that all the time, all the energy, all the effort, all the commitment that it takes to get to be the best, that's the same thing you've got to do every single day just to stay the best. Over the course of the marathon of life, you've got to do those same things every day. That's what makes you successful.

That's it. I hope you enjoyed reading and learning the steps to success and most of all, I really hope you use it. I know if you use it, it will work for you. You will be more successful, and that really is my true reward.

This is Warren Greshes signing off. Make it a great day.

About the Author

Warren Greshes is an expert in sales, motivation and personal, professional and organizational development. This book is taken from Warren's popular radio program *So Who's Stopping You* which ran on AM radio and over the internet on the World Talk Radio Network for two years.

We hope you enjoy this inspiring information about sales, success, customer service and time management from the internationally acclaimed Hall of Fame speaker and top selling author.

Printed in the USA
CPSIA information can be obtained
at www.ICGtesting.com
JSHW012036140824
68134JS00033B/3091

9 781722 500184